Beyond *the* BANK

Beyond the BANK

Hugh McColl's Chapter Two

HOWARD E. COVINGTON JR.

Text © copyright 2021, Howard E. Covington Jr.

All rights reserved. No part of this book may be reproduced or transmitted in any form or by any means, electronic or mechanical, including photocopying, recording, or by any information storage and retrieval system, without written permission from the publisher.

ISBN 978-1-7359622-0-7
Library of Congress Control Number: 2020920503

Editor, Leslie B. Rindoks

Portrait of Hugh L. McColl by Chas Fagan, used with permission.
Printed and bound in the United States of America
First printing March 2021

Published by Lorimer Press

Davidson, NC
www.writingbetterbooks.com

After retiring in 2001,
Hugh L. McColl Jr.,
former chairman and
CEO of Bank of America,
knew he wasn't done
quite yet.

Bank of America employees filled Founders Hall at the bank's corporate center in Uptown Charlotte, North Carolina, on April 25, 2001, to say goodbye to Hugh McColl who arrived wearing his cowboy hat, boots, and jeans and ready to head to his hunting camp in Texas. (From The Charlotte Observer. © 2001 McClatchy. All rights reserved. Used under license.)

TABLE OF CONTENTS

Preface	*ix*
Chapter One, *Social Capital*	*1*
Chapter Two, *A Good Home*	*15*
Chapter Three, *Doing Business*	*33*
Chapter Four, *The Earth Moved*	*57*
Chapter Five, *Raising Money*	*71*
Chapter Six, *Home on the Range*	*89*
Chapter Seven, *Son of the South*	*103*
Chapter Eight, *A Second Legacy*	*125*
Acknowledgments	*143*
Index	*146*

PREFACE

SOME MONTHS back one of Hugh McColl's hunting companions called to introduce himself and suggest that there was a book to be written about his long-time friend. I noted that two books had already been published, one in 1994 and the other in 2000. I co-authored one of them and asked why he thought another was needed now, twenty years after McColl had left the chairman's suite on the 58th floor of the Bank of America tower in Uptown Charlotte.

He encouraged me to answer my own question and a week or so later I was sitting across from McColl in the study of his home. As we talked it became clear that I had been hasty in my judgment and narrow in my thinking. Indeed, there was a book here, just not the one that either of us had in mind. The story this time was not about banking, a story told elsewhere, but McColl certainly had something to say about enjoying a life well lived. High finance would be a part, to be sure, but the story that was resonating quite vigorously was one that was far more personal. It was a story about learning and growth, important components of the essential McColl over the years. This time he was using these remarkable talents to create another form of wealth. He was busy investing in his community what sociologists call social capital.

—Howard E. Covington Jr.
January, 2021

Chapter One
Social Capital

SHAUN CORBETT, a tall Black man with strong shoulders, close-cropped hair, and just the shadow of a close-trimmed beard, stood at the entrance of his LuckySpot Barbershop watching shoppers across the way gather their purchases from the checkout and head for the exit. It was around two p.m. on a Wednesday, and the Walmart Supercenter on Charlotte's west side was busy, indeed very busy for a midweek afternoon—good news for entrepreneurs like Corbett who operate under Walmart's roof.

With the first day of school just ahead in 2019, a hundred kids already had signed up for free back-to-school cuts at LuckySpot. A slender young acolyte named Tim, who began as one of Corbett's apprentices and was now fully licensed, braced for a busy weekend.

Standing there, Corbett believed he was on the cusp of something big. Spread out before him, under the glare of banks of LED ceiling lights, was four acres of retail. LuckySpot is barely a minnow in the Walmart sea, but that's just fine with Corbett because virtually every customer exiting this very big box walks by his shop.

Now, more potential LuckySpot customers pass Corbett's shop in a single day than did over an entire year at his previous northside Charlotte location. In

Shaun Corbett, one of the Black businessmen who gained Hugh McColl's attention, opened LuckySpot Barbershop in a west Charlotte Walmart, with McColl providing pro bono advice and counsel from himself and others.
(Photos courtesy of Michael Graff)

LuckySpot's first week at Walmart, 142 new customers took a chair; 125 in the second. Midway into week three the numbers looked good, and Corbett figured about three-quarters of his old customers had followed him across town.

He had outfitted the space at a minimum of expense. The walls are red, while nearly everything else—the hydraulic chairs and the cabinetry cradling shiny white porcelain sinks—is black. There is room for seven other barbers, and a corner nook has children's books and furniture scaled for knee-high customers. The overall appearance is manly, befitting a barbershop, but women also seek out Lucky for distinctive styling and have for years.

Friends call him Lucky, hence the business's name. The shop's logo features a leprechaun holding a pair of electric hair clippers. (His nickname is tattooed on the left side of his neck, but the collars of his tailored dress shirts obscure most of the ink.)

It was Corbett's civic work—the free back-to-school haircuts and backpacks for kids (more than 2,000 given out one year) and a turkey giveaway at Thanksgiving—that helped convince Walmart executives to give him a lease. Despite a disappointing experiment leasing to hair stylists who catered primarily to women, Walmart was still looking for opportunities to connect with customers and boost "outreach," as the marketing specialists call it. The decision-makers at Walmart's Bentonville, Arkansas, headquarters bought into Corbett's argument that the barbershop is the beating heart of a local community.

No one is more pleased with Corbett's success than his newest best friend and business advisor, Hugh L. McColl Jr. Corbett still couldn't believe that McColl, the retired chairman of Bank of America and a financial titan, was taking him and his business seriously. Whenever Corbett had a question, McColl was as close as his cell phone. When Corbett needed plans drawn to upfit the Walmart space, McColl found an architect who prepared them at no charge. The lawyer who handled lease negotiations also came pro bono, thanks to a couple of phone calls. The man whose bank provided encouragement and billions of dollars in capital to businesses all across the South, on its way to creating one of America's largest financial institutions, was at it again. The prospect of Corbett moving on to claim space in five, ten, or even a hundred or more shops in Walmart locations across the land was no less exciting for McColl than the challenge of rounding up $200 million to bring a National Football League franchise to Charlotte, his hometown. McColl was just operating on a different scale.

Hugh McColl left Bank of America for "retirement" in the spring of 2001. During his forty-plus years in banking he had helped his corporate customers grow and thrive using the leverage of what he always called "his bank," even when he was only a junior officer. In the early days, that was North Carolina National Bank, or NCNB. It reared up in the 1960s with McColl among a pack of aggressive junior bank executives who in a dozen years pushed NCNB ahead of the state's largest institution, Wachovia Bank and Trust Company, a sluggish competitor terminally smug about its portfolio of blue-chip clients.

McColl succeeded to NCNB's chairmanship in 1983 just after the bank outflanked competitors and jumped state lines to access the lucrative markets in Florida. That expansion set off a round of mergers across the South. By 1994, NCNB had become NationsBank, and "McColl's bank" had customers all along the eastern seaboard, from the shores of Miami Beach to the suburbs of Washington, D.C., and as far west as Texas, from El Paso to the lower Rio Grande Valley, where McColl traveled annually to shoot quail. Nearing the end of the century, in 1998, McColl satisfied his ambition for a nationwide franchise when NationsBank acquired BankAmerica, the pride of San Francisco. He made a slight change in the name and installed Bank of America's headquarters smack dab in the center of Charlotte. Making the city an even larger global financial center was a satisfying response to all those who over the years had made fun of southerners as slow, dumb, and awkward—a distasteful stereotype that dogged McColl throughout his professional career.

His record of more than a hundred mergers and acquisitions earned McColl a reputation as a determined competitor who talked tough about "launching his missiles" against those who stood in his way. He wasn't in the business of merging banks; McColl was acquiring them. He closed deals with such regularity that he had a transition team on the road, somewhere, virtually year-round. The coveted reward for successful associates was a crystal hand grenade fashioned after those McColl once tossed out of a training bunker on the Marine Corps range at Quantico, Virginia. He made no apology for the aggressive campaigns he mounted to buy one institution after another. He says it was all in pursuit of building a national franchise. Besides, he declares, it was simply the natural extension of a plan handed him by his predecessors, Addison Reese and Thomas Storrs, NCNB's CEOs in its first twenty-plus years. McColl merely added his own touches to a script he inherited.

McColl's wife, Jane, says all the bluster that business writers spread about her husband is woefully incomplete, leaving him misunderstood. Friends and coworkers confirm her opinion. All in all, McColl has always been a soft touch for a stranger with a hard-luck story, and he is ever willing to shed cash or sweat, whichever is required at the time, in aid of a "teammate" or anyone he considers in need. It's true that he's not much on small talk and can be a bit brusque. He also becomes prickly at situations he deems unjust, unreasonable, discriminatory, or just plain silly. Basically, he values loyalty and honesty, and he adheres to a simple credo, one he learned in the Marine Corps's officer training, that can apply to a corporation or a community:

take care of your people, they'll take care of the customers, and that will satisfy the shareholders.

When the vaunted Business Roundtable, America's top-tier of corporate CEOs, declared midway through 2019 that shareholder profits should not be the only purpose of business, McColl was incredulous. He had lived by much broader and more compassionate values for years. "One of the most crucial elements of leadership is actually caring about other people," he once told an interviewer. It was why his team was willing to crash through brick walls (and state lines) on his behalf. It was clear as day to him that a leader's downfall always came when they quit taking care of those by their side.

McColl was well compensated while at the bank, though not as richly as some operating at his level. When he left, virtually his entire fortune was in Bank of America stock. In order to avoid real or perceived conflicts of interest, he had never spread his investments around. He only began making what Wall Streeters would call real money after he was on his own. His annual take-home pay tripled to about $15 million after he created McColl Partners, a mergers and acquisitions firm that was licensed to do business September 10, 2001. The Great Recession in 2009 later took a huge bite out of his wealth, but he recovered in the years that followed thanks to a successful turn of investments from his partnership in the private-equity firm, Falfurrias Capital.

> He enjoys making money because it means he has more of it to give away.

Some rich men say money is their way of keeping score. McColl claims he enjoys making money because it means he has more of it to give away. A remarkable record of fund-raising in Charlotte is testimony to his generosity. So was a sizable tip he left for a luncheon waitress one day. The extra was not to impress his guest but given with the knowledge that the server needed the $20 more than he did.

Even as McColl accumulated wealth and power, he and Jane never saw the need to upgrade a lifestyle that had suited them for years. They had bought a handsome brick Georgian-style two-story in 1992 and were still living in the same well-to-do Charlotte neighborhood nearly thirty years later. The house is big, but nothing like the McMansions popular in his part of town. The interior is well-appointed and serves as a gallery of sorts for favorite pieces of art chosen from a collection that the two have accumulated over the years. Hugh's favorites are maritime scenes. His real excess is a South Texas hunting camp with a low-slung lodge and a full-time staff. The foremen and his men look after about 1,000 head of cattle grazing on roughly 40,000 acres spread across the flatlands eighty miles north of the border town of Brownsville.

McColl's everyday tastes are simple. He dresses casually and favors black T-shirts, Levi jeans held up by a belt with a silver ram's head buckle (he is a graduate of the University of North Carolina), and comfortable leather sport shoes (also in black). He drives a BMW sport utility vehicle. (He shifted from black to cream.) A 1993 Ford Ranger pickup that looks like it has been disguised as an abandoned vehicle stays parked in back of the house. Among the stickers literally covering the tailgate is one that reads, "YOU MAY ALL GO TO HELL AND I WILL GO TO TEXAS –DAVY CROCKETT." ANOTHER: "I GOT THIS TRUCK FOR MY WIFE—GOOD TRADE, HUH?"

Growing old hasn't been easy. Not long after doctors repaired his rotator cuff, injured during a pickup basketball game, at age sixty-nine McColl underwent heart bypass surgery. A decade later he had to learn to walk again after brain surgery. It took months of physical therapy before McColl regained full mobility. Yoga and continued physical therapy restored him to health, although he now walks with a side-to-side motion slightly reminiscent of a penguin's gait. He is happy to note that today he can swing his custom Spanish-made .20-gauge shotgun into shooting position as smoothly as he ever did before doctors opened up his skull.

A single medical event, not to mention two, would have convinced most old warriors that it was time to turn things over to a younger set, not McColl.

He was forced to face the real possibility of dying, however, as an ambulance rushed him to Charlotte from the clubhouse at Augusta National, where he had collapsed in December 2014. "I just thought that was it," he would later allow. Jane tells him that he's still alive for a purpose. Hugh says he's not so sure and changes the subject, but he adds, "Yeah, it changed my life. I guess I decided to live."

The fact of the matter is that facing death, with resignation or not, can focus one's attention. In the years following that long ambulance ride to Charlotte across South Carolina on Interstate 85, McColl has increased his commitment to addressing some of Charlotte's deepest problems. High on the agenda has been the yawning gaps of economic disparity between whites and Blacks. Urban riots in September 2016 moved him to begin to do more than think about problems, to do more than talk about them. The Black Lives Matter movement reinforced his resolve.

For McColl, Charlotte is not simply the place where he lives. It is who he is. Charlotte and McColl came of age together. A sleepy burg back in the sixties that out-of-towners never could place correctly—*Is it in North Carolina or South Carolina?*—Charlotte, North Carolina was where he and Jane began raising their family. The bank he worked for was young, too, at least in name, and as eager to build a record as McColl was to make something of himself. When he had the chance, McColl began investing the bank's money, and a considerable amount of his own time and attention, in rebuilding the city's center. McColl can honestly claim to have built much of what's called Uptown Charlotte when he directed the investment of hundreds of millions of his bank's money

> High on his agenda has been the economic disparity between whites and Blacks.

When Hugh McColl and Braxton Winston first met they tangled over a touchy racial question. A few months later McColl was the first person Winston called to tell he was beginning what proved to be a winning campaign for an at-large seat on the Charlotte City Council in 2017. He was reelected in 2019. (Photo by Matthew Tyndall. Courtesy of Braxton Winston)

into new buildings and projects in the center city. They grew side by side, and by the twenty-first century no other single individual had left such an imprint. Just as Bank of America was "his bank," Charlotte was "his town."

One of the nation's urban growth centers, Charlotte's trajectory continued into the twenty-first century with an amazing record of expansion and prosperity. By the 2010s, the number of newcomers alone equaled the population of a small city, about 45,000 people, arriving every year or so. It became a marvel on almost any scale—jobs, population, per capita income—and home to *Fortune* 500 companies, sports teams, and cultural amenities. In the new century, the city's Uptown skyline continued to be reshaped by new office towers and high-rise apartment buildings. Even in the midst of the Covid-19 pandemic in early 2020, Centene, one of the nation's largest insurers, announced it planned to spend $1 billion over twelve years to build out an eighty-acre campus where as many as 6,000 employees could work one day.

All that prosperity was not spread evenly over the city, now a metropolitan area with a population of 1.2 million. Charlotte suffers from a legacy of racial differences that dull the city's shine. In 2001, sociologist Robert Putnam reported appallingly low levels of trust between whites and Blacks in Charlotte. More recently, in 2014, celebrated economist Raj Chetty and a team of researchers from Stanford mined a vast quantity of data points to define the extent of the city's crippling lack of upward mobility. Data from a fifty-city study showed that children born Black, poor, or both in Charlotte or Mecklenburg County were most likely to remain at the bottommost economic tier for the rest of their lives.

Racial separation and lack of opportunity ignited outrage following the death of a Black man shot by Charlotte police in September 2016. The event produced nights of protests as National Guard troops and tear gas savaged Charlotte's image. The consequences went deep and shocked people from their complacency. The events troubled McColl, and he turned his time and attention to learning more about himself and his neighbors. It also set him on a journey that would eventually lead to LuckySpot and Shaun Corbett.

One of McColl's friends at city hall told him about Corbett and the favorable attention the barber was receiving for his civic work, including a program called Cops

& Barbers, which brings police officers and young men from the community together in the barbershop where they have a chance to talk frankly and honestly. The Obama White House heard about the program in 2015 and invited Corbett to travel there twice, once for a panel on twenty-first-century policing and a second time with Charlotte police chief Kerr Putney. McColl's friend suggested that he might lend Corbett a hand with some of his business plans.

McColl thought everyone who lived in Charlotte had probably heard of him. In the twenty years since he'd left Bank of America, he had remained a media favorite. Leaders in politics, business, and the arts called on him for everything.

Shaun Corbett, busy sorting out his own future, must have missed all that Uptown Charlotte news because when a stranger called him out of the blue asking about his vision for LuckySpot, Corbett had no idea who he was talking to.

Corbett nearly choked on his biscuit when McColl said something about owning Bojangles'. The shambling old white guy meant his investment firm owned every one of Bojangles' six hundred stores, not the one lone franchise on the north side of Charlotte where they were talking about Corbett's future.

Six months earlier, in August 2018, David Taylor, the executive of the Gantt Center for African-American Arts + Culture, arranged for two other barbers, twin brothers, Damian and Jermaine Johnson, to visit McColl at his office on the forty-first floor of the Bank of America Corporate Center. The outing to McColl's office was mostly to satisfy Taylor's goal of putting a couple of enterprising Black businessmen in front of McColl. It was supposed to be a fifteen-minute meet and greet. The session went on for more than an hour.

Damian was thrilled. He had admired the retired banker from afar and was eager to go. "If you get an opportunity to sit at the foot of a giant," he said, "that was more than enough."

His brother, Jermaine, wasn't all that impressed. Like Corbett, McColl's name just didn't register. Thinking McColl was a politician, Jermaine couldn't understand why some stranger, a white guy no less, was interested in him and Damian. Maybe McColl could have helped them in the past, but now? They were doing all right. At the time, their operation included five shops, plus a barber school, and they were on their way to expanding with more locations in South Carolina and Georgia. Before the meeting, he did a little research and found McColl on a couple of YouTube videos. "He's direct," Jermaine said later. "I liked that."

The brothers, who are in their mid-forties but could pass for fifteen years younger, showed up at McColl's office wearing complementary outfits set off with bow ties. Taylor began to describe to McColl what the Johnsons had created. Their host interrupted. "Let them tell it," he said.

> " It made me look at America different"
> —Damian Johnson

Barbers can spin a yarn; it's in their DNA. McColl can talk to a post. Within minutes, the three had connected. McColl was intrigued with the brothers' ambition to grow their business into a chain of NoGrease! establishments. (The name refers to a barber's aversion to customers with oily hair.) McColl immediately understood that they had a complete package, with the barber school serving as a career on-ramp for young Black men as well as an important manpower stream for future expansion. (Shaun Corbett, who had delivered pizzas late at night to earn enough to pay for his training, was one of their graduates.)

The three men talked about family, race, and the legacies of the segregated South, as well as the struggles Black businessmen face. They covered money, power, and family coincidences. (The Johnsons' grandfather shared the same birthdate as McColl, June 18.) As the conversation flowed, Damian thought he saw McColl recalibrating long-held assumptions about people like him and his brother.

"It was a beautiful thing," he recalled, "because he was literally trying to figure it out right then. He had a moment, and we did too. I have never sat in front of a white guy who's done the things he's done. I never even thought he'd even try to give any thought to how to help Black people. [And now] I saw him thinking about his past decisions and how he could have helped Black people or how he thought he was helping Black people, but the help didn't get to guys like us. You can see he had been thinking about that.

"Being a Black man who's grown up in America and seeing powerful white guys as 'Ah, they don't think about us,' I saw him sitting there trying to think about it. It made me look at, not just white people, but it made me look at America different. That was a different moment."

McColl tossed out the names of a few of Charlotte's top Black business executives but the names meant no more to the Johnsons than McColl's had to Jermaine hours before. Said Damian, "I know Black guys who are in those circles who wouldn't dare travel in the circles I travel in." Then he told McColl, "Right now, you're Blacker than them to me. We just don't know those guys. It was definitely his ah-ha moment and definitely mine. That could be a problem, that could be something that we are missing."

Jermaine remained skeptical. He just didn't believe a one percenter like McColl could begin to appreciate wealth the same as a Black man, particularly one half his age. "You know, here I am. I ain't got two nickels to rub if I had to compare," Jermaine said. "Then he said this: 'We want the same thing.' And I'm like, let me hear this. Let's hear what this sounds like."

McColl continued: "I want power, and not that I want power over anybody, I just don't want anybody to have power over me." Jermaine remembers, "I sat back, and said, 'We do want the same thing. We want the same thing.' He said it wasn't about money. It was about being self-empowered. That right there—Boy, when I got that right there, that's what I came for."

The session was about to end when McColl put a question to them. What big dream did they have? Damian said he envisioned Charlotte developing a thriving Black community highlighting Black culture, food, and entertainment. "I believe you could make that happen," McColl told him. Jermaine, still pondering the lesson on power, was more pragmatic. "Share our story with someone else."

McColl did just that. He was troubled that the brothers were saddled with an expansion loan that came with an outrageous interest rate. They hadn't asked for him to do a thing on their behalf, but the situation nagged. He asked Jermaine for his phone number and told him he'd be in touch. An hour later, Johnson's phone rang, and he heard a voice. "This is Hugh McColl. I am going to have some people [from Bank of America] call you within the hour. Just tell them what you told me about your business plan, and they're going to help you out."

"Yes, sir. Thank you."

"Don't thank me. Just keep doing what you're doing."

By the end of the day, a loan officer called to request a copy of a Small Business Administration application to refinance the brothers' $300,000 debt. They had been working on their financing and SBA approval for months. One bank had put a deal on the table, but the brothers' steady cash flow history and demonstrated record of repayment still resulted in less than ideal terms. All the more galling was that the offer came from the state's largest Black-owned bank.

Thirty days later the Johnsons moved their note to Bank of America with an interest rate a third of what they had been paying. They wrote McColl a year later, and recalling their first meeting, they told him the money they had saved with the lower interest rate, nearly $30,000 annually, was going toward the purchase of the building where they had opened their first NoGrease! twenty-two years ago.

McColl sloughs off attempts to get him to acknowledge his efforts on their behalf. It had taken very little to do what he did. "They didn't know how to take it to the next step," he said. "[What I did] is being part of the white male club. It's about knowing who to call," says the man with coast-to-coast contacts. Punching in ten digits on his cell phone can put him in touch with most anyone, from Warren Buffett to Barack Obama to Bill Gates.

McColl has so many stories like this that he has forgotten many of them. A history of opening doors, providing "access," as McColl calls it, has always been part of who he is, what he does. Today, social scientists have another name for it. They tout the potential of using "social capital" to enhance upward mobility and make communities more equitable. Put simply, McColl said one wintry day in 2019, "What I am doing these days is spending time trying to figure out how to help people."

Making connections. That's really what's on McColl's agenda. The faces change, but the conversation is almost always the same. Earlier that day, he was at the office of the president of Central Piedmont Community College, where they were talking about job training. "We know that education, practical education, is important." Jobs produce incomes; incomes make house payments and educate children. "Our system is not working," he said. "We're leaving more and more people behind. People with money have gotten richer by staggering yardage, and people without capital have never been poorer. We can't sustain this as a nation. You eventually have a revolution.

"After three years of working on it I'm convinced that jobs are the only answer, the only quick answer. The only way you can lift people is by training them to have a job and then giving them the job and letting them then take charge of their lives. You give them pride, of course, because they got a job they can handle themselves. They're not on the dole to anybody."

That conviction has led him to people like Corbett and the Johnsons and also to Ric Elias. He's about the same age as the Johnsons but operates on a much grander scale. His company, Red Ventures, is a multinational portfolio of digital companies that runs from a campus just across the state line in South Carolina. Red Ventures has more than 3,000 employees, but Elias is no less in awe of McColl than Shaun Corbett.

Elias came to the United States from Puerto Rico, mastered English, and went from Boston College to a Harvard MBA. He founded his company in 2000, and within seven years was ranked fourth on the Inc. 500 list of the fastest-growing companies in America. He tells a compelling story about surviving the so-called Miracle on the Hudson as a passenger on Flight 1549, which crash-landed onto the Hudson River alongside New York City. His TED Talk has received nearly 7.5 million views. The three things he learned that day include: (1) everything changes in an instant, so don't postpone anything, (2) eliminate negative energy, and (3) the only thing that matters is being a good dad. "The gift for me that day was seeing into the future and being about to come back and live differently," he told his TED audience in 2011.

McColl is taken with Elias and his creation of a job-training program called Road2Hire, which has the capacity to provide well-paid jobs for thousands of young people. McColl's challenge: persuading a highly successful entrepreneur of the value of collaborative philanthropy. Elias says of his new friend, "There are not many cities where you have a figure who is so impactful and influential. He is a Rockefeller, a J. P. Morgan, a captain of the city."

McColl's minister, Bob Henderson, says, "I find him in many ways to be a positive example of how to live fully alive." McColl brushes such praise aside. "What I'm trying to do now are things I can do as opposed to attacking something I can't fix," McColl says. "I've learned at eighty-four that I can't change the world, but we can change the outlook for one person or ten people or twenty people. I'm trying to deal with the world that I'm able to deal with.

"But one of the things I'm wrestling with at the moment is whether my caring matters, if you follow me? Whether I'm just wasting time. Although I don't know what I'd do with the time otherwise. That, I believe, is one of the biggest problems of old age, is what to do with the time? That's an interesting problem."

CHAPTER TWO
A Good Home

CHARLOTTE'S WASHINGTON Heights, created in 1913 as one of the first "streetcar suburbs" for middle-income African Americans, was sited on the high ground west of downtown. White developers touted this new neighborhood as the Black equivalent of Myers Park, the white-only subdivision with large lots and curving streets southeast of the city where lots had gone on sale two years earlier.

Named in recognition of the leading Black educator of the day, Booker T. Washington, the neighborhood further underscored his importance with the naming of Booker Street. Booker Street was cut wider to accommodate an anticipated extension of the city trolley line whose western terminus was nearby. Biddle Institute (later Johnson C. Smith University) was close also. Another new street was Sanders Avenue, which may have been named in honor of Biddle's first president, D. J. Sanders. Prime lots fronting Beatties Ford Road, the main thoroughfare running along the eastern edge of the Heights, sold for $500 each. They carried deed covenants that houses would cost no less than $1,000.

Washington Heights' developer, W. S. Alexander, promised cement sidewalks, graded streets, a plentiful supply of water from artesian wells, "and every convenience possible." The September 1912 announcement in the *Charlotte Daily Observer* presented an image of suburban life previously available only to Charlotte's white residents. (Alexander had developed white neighborhoods such as Elizabeth on Charlotte's near east side and Western Heights, also on Beatties Ford Road.) In Washington Heights, homeowners could be assured of an all-residential enclave and the freshness of the countryside with freedom from undesirable neighbors like machine shops or billiard parlors. There was talk of amenities to come, including a baseball park and an auditorium and dancing pavilion exclusively for African Americans.

C. H. Watson, a prominent Black businessman, handled sales at Washington Heights and already had a stake in the neighborhood's success; he owned the pavilions at the end of the main trolley line that were available to weekend picnickers.

According to the newspaper, "far-sighted men" believed Brooklyn, the Black neighborhood then located in Charlotte's southeast Second Ward, "must sooner or later be utilized by the white population." Making a case for developing Washington Heights, the paper said: "It is the opinion quite generally held among white citizens of Charlotte that the solution of the question of housing the colored population for the best interest of all is afforded by the sites west of the city, where the educational center is already established."

Washington Heights developed slowly. The park promised at the outset never materialized, but another, Clinton Park, opened nearby in the mid-1920s. Not far from the end of the trolley line and close to Stewart Creek, the park had a dance hall and a swimming area with diving platforms. Its bathhouse boasted one hundred changing rooms. On a hot Sunday afternoon in September 1926, an estimated 5,000 African Americans and a handful of whites gathered at the water's edge to be baptized, or watch those being dunked. Over the course of three-plus hours that afternoon, Bishop Charles Manuel "Sweet Daddy" Grace of the House of Prayer and Church of the Rock received 643 souls in the name of the Lord. Two weeks later, with a crowd twice as large, another 700 or so were baptized. Sadly, one of Grace's deacons drowned while trying to save a woman when she attempted to cross the deeper reaches of the swimming area. (She was rescued unharmed by another worshipper.)

As Charlotte grew, so did the population on the city's west side. In time, subdivisions such as University Park, McCrorey Heights, Biddle Heights, and Hyde Park filled in the blank space along Beatties Ford Road. West Charlotte High School opened nearby in 1938 and became the pride of the community. (It would later figure prominently in the racial integration of Charlotte's public schools.) Bishop Grace built A House of Prayer for All People on Beatties Ford Road. A movie theater, locally owned eateries, and a variety of businesses cropped up. They were joined in 1944 by a popular night spot called the Excelsior Club that would attract some of the best-known Black entertainers in the land.

As it happened, Brooklyn thrived for another fifty years, all the while supporting a concentration of Black-owned businesses and churches. Charlotte's first high school for African Americans was located there, along with some upscale homes. Regrettably, the area also produced the city's worst slums, a feature that became the foundation of the argument at city hall to have Brooklyn scraped bare between 1960 and 1968. So-called urban renewal was underway as Hugh McColl settled into his job at Charlotte's new bank, and it forced the relocation away from downtown of more than a thousand families, over two hundred businesses, and a dozen or so houses of worship. In the sixties, the white establishment didn't bother to suggest to the Second Ward diaspora that a good life awaited the displaced in the suburbs. Those who were required to move were on their own to find another place to live.

By the end of the twentieth century, however, Washington Heights was suffering from decline and neglect. The last new homes had been built in the early 1960s, and the population stagnated. Highway engineers trimmed away a portion for the construction of a freeway. In 1990, the attempted murder of eight men, reminiscent of gangland violence from Chicago, horrified everyone. Couples who once took walks together in the evening now stayed inside after dark with their doors locked.

In 1999, Bank of America had financed a revolving fund to help a neighborhood association build Washington Heights' first new houses in more than thirty years. Two years later, bank executive Lynn Drury made a pass through the neighborhood. She, along with others who worked closely with Hugh McColl, were on a mission, eager to complete the details of a unique retirement gift for their boss. Rather than give him a gold watch or some fancy remembrance that would probably be shoved in a desk drawer and forgotten, the bank's board of directors planned to underwrite the construction of more than 200 houses through Habitat for Humanity. This generous gesture, which could cost $10 million or more, called for volunteers to build the first ten houses on vacant lots in Washington Heights.

Drury believed the project would appeal to McColl. It recognized years of effort that he had devoted to Habitat, a favorite nonprofit enterprise that combined elements he found meaningful. He liked the cooperative efforts of volunteers, many of whom arrived on a job site as strangers and became fast friends. He liked the participation of prospective homeowners who invested their own sweat, putting in hours, hammer in hand, with others in order to realize their dream. He liked the notion that this wasn't a giveaway. Homeowners accepted the responsibility of long-term mortgages and were expected to keep their payments current.

McColl had long believed that home ownership was a cornerstone of every community. Neighborhoods thrived when people were invested in the place where they lived. They put down roots, got to know their neighbors, and raised families secure in the knowledge that their growing home equity could someday help pay for a child's college education or be used to start or grow a business. In his years leading the bank, McColl spoke often about the importance of getting an education, finding a job, and enjoying the rewards of home ownership.

Over the years, McColl's bank had put its money where McColl's mouth was. When federal bank regulators were considering the proposed merger of NCNB and C&S/Sovran in 1991, a combination that produced NationsBank, McColl promised to make $10 billion available to low- and moderate-income borrowers over ten years. It was a huge investment. In comparison, when President Bill Clinton announced plans to infuse money into communities across the entire nation, the federal government's pledge was a paltry $350 million. NationsBank invested nearly thirty times that amount in the southeastern United States. A $500 million slice of that went to help the working poor who couldn't afford a down payment. There was also money available for renovations.

NationsBank was just a few years into this massive lending program when community activists claimed banks were slighting poor and Black neighborhoods. They lit up South Tryon Street with brilliant yellow T-shirts bearing the slogan "Stop The Loan Sharks." One of the protest leaders, Bruce Marks of the Neighborhood Assistance Corporation of America, was spending a lot of time in the city, leading picketers in front of the headquarters of NationsBank as well as at First Union National Bank, McColl's main competitor, just down the street.

Catherine Bessant was the NationsBank executive who had come up with the $10 billion program, and McColl had put her in charge of making it work. By 1995 most of the bank's $10 billion program had been dispersed and was already in the hands of borrowers, but Marks continued to protest on the plaza in front of McColl's building as bank mergers proceeded apace. He demanded that Bessant arrange a sit-down with bank officials.

McColl gave her a lesson she would never forget.

Marks, walking with a group of protesters carrying posters, was outside the bank entrance when McColl, in his shirtsleeves, walked out the door and asked him what he wanted. Unaware who he was speaking to, Marks said that no one inside would talk to him face-to-face. "Well, you're talking to the chairman of the damn bank," McColl responded. "You want to talk? Come upstairs."

That session was the first of several and eventually Marks found himself in partnership with the bank. He worked to shape lending programs that provided money for unsophisticated borrowers eager to take advantage of new opportunities. McColl's gambit infuriated the leadership at First Union. Marks now focused all of his protests there; the battle was over at NationsBank. A few years later, Marks and his fellow activists testified in favor of the NationsBank acquisition of BankAmerica. Some of those who spoke at a public hearing held by regulators were new homeowners. They talked about living their dream because NationsBank had kept its word in its lending program.

Twenty years later, Bessant still keeps a copy of Saul Alinsky's handbook for protest, *Rules for Radicals*, in her desk drawer. Her triumphs with community development and managing change had won her an office on the fifty-eighth floor of Bank of America's Corporate Center, just down the corridor from McColl's successor, chairman and CEO Brian T. Moynihan. Bessant looked back fondly on those early years and said her work remains her avocation. When she proved she could keep regulators happy, create new homeowners and new bank customers, and produce profits all at the same time, she was assured of one of McColl's crystal grenades.

On McColl's way out the door in 2001, he made another big pot of money available for this special lending program. This time the bank allocated $350 billion to its investment in low- and moderate-income lending.

> "It became an arms race with other banks… the best kind of arms race to have."
> —Catherine Bessant

"The $350 billion was set up to be a ten-year goal," Bessant remembers, "and I think we did it in six. The purpose was to get ahead of debate and discussion as opposed to behind it. It became indisputable that we were the leader because everything that we did was enveloped by the big, bold commitment that nobody in either case had ever made before. It became a little bit of an arms race then with other banks, but that's the best kind of arms race to have. That never bothered Hugh. It never bothered me. What could be better than daring Citigroup or daring J. P. Morgan to have to make a big commitment, too?"

NationsBank was one of the most generous and regular contributors to the Charlotte Habitat affiliate when McColl retired. In making plans for her boss's departure, Lynn Drury had first suggested that all of the bank-sponsored Habitat homes be built in Charlotte. The local affiliate was one of the most active and successful in the country, and the McColl build would enhance its reputation even more. As it happened, no one was interested in concentrating a hundred Habitat houses in one location, and finding dispersed sites for that many houses was problematic. That wasn't the way the organization worked.

The solution then became obvious: extend the McColl Habitat Project across the nation and build houses in each of the twenty-one U.S. states and Latin American countries where Bank of America did business. When McColl heard about the plans on his behalf, he called it "the highest honor that he could imagine." He told a newspaper reporter, "This is the best retirement present I could imagine, and the fun part is that so many people get to share in it."

The plan was announced in December 2001, a few months after McColl had transitioned into retirement. It was formally launched in April 2002, with the first sites chosen for new homes in Washington Heights. There was a public declaration that teams of volunteers in Charlotte would complete the first ten houses in thirty days in an ecumenical effort. Bank of America paid all the expenses, but McColl insisted that volunteer labor be recruited from the other banks; Queens University, where he chaired the board of trustees; his fellow church members at Covenant Presbyterian; and other community organizations. As a result, building teams composed of people from all across the city turned out over the course of four successive weekends, working Thursdays through Saturdays to meet the deadline.

Much about this project was different from the way things had been done before, including the design of the homes. For years, Habitat houses built in Charlotte had all looked pretty much alike. They were one-story frame structures covered in vinyl siding and ranged in size from two to four bedrooms. They sat on concrete slabs, with the front door in a modest recessed stoop cut into one corner. These homes were functional, inexpensive, and generally unattractive. Everything about them declared they were low-cost housing for people of modest means.

The people in Washington Heights were proud of their history and the style of their homes. A number of the early ones were still standing. The old style was frame bungalows with hip roofs, broad eaves, and exposed rafter ends. This one-story model was carried forward in many of the houses built in later years. Nearly all of them had one thing in common: porches. They spread across the fronts of the houses, and some wrapped around to one side. This was true even for some of the brick ranches built in the 1950s.

Habitat's standard houses didn't have porches; Washington Heights and its residents said that wouldn't do. Unwilling to get off to a bad start, the Habitat organization worked with architects and engineers to arrive at a new house style that borrowed from the old Craftsman model and came complete with a porch. That pleased everyone. The change pushed the cost over the initial budget estimate of $50,000 per house, but no one seemed to mind.

Drury recruited Brenda L. Suits from the bank's corporate audit department to run the project. Suits and McColl had been working together on a NationsBank Habitat building team for more than fifteen years. Back in 1988, young, impetuous, and energetic, she took a flyer and called McColl's office with an invitation to join a Habitat team. Suits had a sense that McColl would want to be involved. A year earlier he had helped the Charlotte affiliate raise money to underwrite a building project that brought former president Jimmy Carter and his wife, Rosalynn, to Charlotte for a week. She was in her twenties then, but she had more tenure than her age implied, having started her employment as a teenager working summers in the bank's operations center. After earning a business and accounting degree from the University of North Carolina at Greensboro in 1983, she joined the bank's management program. When she issued her invite, her only contact with McColl had been a passing introduction in an elevator when he stuck his hand out and said, "Hi, I'm Hugh McColl." He did that a lot.

When she called the chairman's office, she understood that McColl was a very busy man, so she wasn't surprised when his assistant, Pat Hinson, called to say McColl was due to arrive in Charlotte late the night before the Habitat build, having just completed a journey halfway around the world. Mr. McColl wouldn't be in shape to report to a work site at seven a.m., Suits was told.

Thirty years later, Suits exudes a degree of confidence and purpose that explains how she earned her stripes. She's still a Habitat volunteer when she's in town and not on the road handling assignments for the Bank of America Foundation, where she is now a senior vice president. That call to McColl was for a "blitz build." That's what Habitat calls an unbelievable amount of work completed by an overwhelming army of volunteers in a remarkably short period of time. Suits was not surprised at Hinson's message, but was taken aback when she arrived at the building site forty-five minutes before the work whistle was to blow, and was told her boss was on the ground and looking for her.

McColl shook off his jetlag and worked with the bank's team throughout the day before quitting at four p.m. when another crew arrived to continue construction on into the night. Everyone was expected back the next morning for the house dedication. During his shift, McColl handled all manner of tasks, doing whatever came his way. At one point a Habitat supervisor approached David Walker, a member of the bank team, and said he had heard that McColl was some kind of big shot at NCNB. "Yeah, he's our chairman and CEO," Walker replied. "Oh, great," he was told, "I've got him fetching toilets."

McColl left the work site at the end of that first day only to return around three a.m. or so, running on a reservoir of adrenaline. The crew was pushing to finish by daybreak, and McColl was on a roof nailing shingles when he began slipping over the surface slick with dew. Fortunately, someone stopped his slide or NCNB's CEO might have been recuperating in the hospital when the house was dedicated.

The first day of that 1988 build, over bologna sandwiches, Suits asked McColl to consider enrolling NCNB in a Habitat program called "Adopt a Home." It was something new for organizations and companies that wanted to provide the labor and money for construction of a single house. He readily agreed, and NCNB's check for $40,000 paid for the first Habitat house in Charlotte built entirely with corporate support.

That house was in Optimist Park, a distressed neighborhood just north of downtown. A century before, the area had been home to white families whose breadwinners worked in the construction trades or had jobs at nearby Alpha Mill, one of Charlotte's first textile mills. When Habitat began building houses there in 1987, Optimist Park was struggling. Existing housing was substandard, and the population, once all white, had transitioned to almost all Black. The change had begun in the late 1950s and then accelerated in the 1960s when African Americans displaced from Brooklyn came looking for low-cost housing. Unemployment and crime were both high. Hope was pretty low.

Habitat concentrated its early efforts in Optimist Park, and NCNB's house was part of this effort. Over two weeks, volunteers from various departments took shifts to complete the work. McColl was on site whenever he could find the time. One day he was taking a break with others when a woman approached and introduced herself. She lived in a Habitat house just up the street, and said she worked at NCNB. Hearing that, McColl asked why she wasn't lending a hand to support her teammates and improve life for a neighbor-to-be. She told him she worked the night shift at the bank's operations center and usually slept during the day. McColl then learned the woman was supporting herself, her child, and a parent on her salary. He commented on the difficulty of her tough schedule and entry level pay, but she told him, "I've got to work my way up. I've got to put in my time."

As folks' attention drifted elsewhere, McColl stepped away to find a phone. In a few minutes, Suits saw him walking up the street to the woman's house. She learned later that McColl had arranged for the woman to work a daytime schedule beginning the following week. "He was always looking out for people," Suits said. Even when bank teams weren't busy, Suits would be out on a Habitat build and see McColl arrive on foot, walking down streets that she was sure his security detail at the bank would never approve of. "He really did care about these neighborhoods and these areas within our city."

The McColl build's first project, the one in Washington Heights, concluded in mid-May 2002 with a celebration organized by Suits that included a parade through the neighborhood with the Johnson C. Smith University band leading the way. There were prayers and food aplenty, and a circle of volunteers led a Bible presentation as each of the ten houses was dedicated. A center of activity for much of that day, as it had been for most of the previous month, was Tabernacle Baptist Church on Redbud Street. The handsome church, a single story of cream-colored brick with a tall white steeple, had opened its doors for volunteers to make and serve lunchtime sandwiches so workers could find some shade and restrooms. Back in 1994, when residents were still dealing with the daily threats to their safety, neighborhood residents had gathered in that church to raise their complaints to city hall about the neglected state of their community. Things were on the uptick now.

Jane McColl joined her husband for the celebration. At one point during the day, with the dedication ceremonies moving from house to house, the two of them pulled away in Hugh's stickered pickup truck in search of a furniture store. Jane, an Old South girl, believed that a front porch wasn't much of a front porch without a rocking chair. Her opinion made for one very happy salesman who wrote an order that afternoon for twenty rocking chairs, two for each porch.

Habitat frowns on volunteers making personal gifts. That had never stopped McColl, whose spontaneity could completely change the conversation. One day, on

Pegram Street in Optimist Park, Suits figured she must have made him mad when he left the work site without saying a word of goodbye. He returned a little later with a basketball goal and backboard in the trunk of his car. A couple of teammates followed him up the street, where they removed a rickety metal rim that the neighborhood Michael Jordans were using and installed the new equipment. McColl stuck around to break in the new basket with the kids before he buckled on his tool belt and returned to work.

Patricia Mackey became a new Washington Heights homeowner on the dedication day, May 11, 2002. Her house, across from Tabernacle Baptist, is directly behind the Habitat home that belongs to her mother on the corner of Redbud and Dundeen. Mackey's mother had insisted the two go through the Habitat application process together, hoping to leave behind the small, crowded apartment where her daughter lived with her three children.

Seventeen years later Mackey and her mother were still in their homes; the rocking chairs still on their porches. Patricia works as a certified nurse's assistant at the nursing home where her mother was the supervisor of housekeeping before she retired. She and her mother are both looking forward to the day coming soon when their homes will be paid for. Yes, she said, she remembers Hugh and Jane McColl. Still pictured in her mind is Jane waiting patiently in the cab of the truck while her husband cleared poison ivy off the trunk of tall gum tree at the edge of her yard.

Another incident that day remained with Suits. The celebration was underway, and McColl was standing with his family—his daughter and her children—when a woman began to question him about Habitat. She didn't know who McColl was but figured he was in charge, what with all the attention he was getting. She wanted to know how homeowners qualified for a house. How much did it cost? Who was eligible? McColl answered her questions, one by one, until she finally allowed that she'd probably never qualify because she had a pile of unpaid medical bills. McColl then became the one asking questions. The woman had come with Jenelle Lozano, one of the regulars on the bank's Habitat crew. Jenelle, whose husband, Juan, was also a bank employee, was mentoring the woman as part of a prison ministry. He asked Jenelle to call him the next day.

Jenelle outlined the challenges her mentee faced while trying to get her life back together. That was enough for McColl, who saw that Jenelle got money to clear the woman's debt so she could qualify for a house. Approval wasn't immediate, but she subsequently moved into her own home, unaware that her benefactor was the short guy in blue jeans whom she happened to chat up one day when a marching band led a parade through Washington Heights.

After the launch in Charlotte, the McColl Habitat Building Project continued for five years. McColl was involved the entire time, traveling to around sixty cities and towns to build houses, including two weeklong trips to Mexico. He was not the sort to show up for the launch and then lose interest until the closing ceremony rolled around. The bank's plane flew Suits, McColl, and a team of volunteers to some Habitat work site virtually every month. They usually stayed for two days or more, longer when working in the further reaches of Mexico with teammates from Santander, a Mexican bank partially owned by Bank of America.

For McColl, building Habitat houses with bank associates all across the country was a "five-year love-in."

Bank of America Foundation executive Brenda L. Suits, second from right, kept Hugh McColl and a team of volunteers on the road for five years building some of the more than 200 Habitat for Humanity houses that Bank of America sponsored in honor of its retired chief executive. With him on a building site in Texas were (left to right) Don Bechtol, Juan Lozano, Kim Braswell, David Vickers-Koch, McColl, Suits, and David Walker. (Photo courtesy of Juan Lozano)

They turned out regardless of conditions. One of the early work sites was in Sumter, South Carolina, and Suits suffered through the outbound leg with McColl grumbling about the use of a fancy corporate jet when they could easily have made the two-hour drive from Charlotte. After they spent the day in the broiling sun with only a borrowed undertaker's tent for protection, McColl welcomed the comfort of a rich man's ride to get him back home. (That day, the crew began with about thirty-nine volunteers; only six remained on the job site at day's end.) On another occasion, Suits, McColl, and the team arrived in Memphis wearing shorts and T-shirts to find the local temperature near freezing. On the way to the job site, they stopped at a Kmart where McColl scooped up sweatshirts bargain-priced at three for ten dollars. In the fall of 2005, McColl, recovering from shoulder surgery with his left arm in a sling, turned up in Texas to show he could still swing a hammer.

McColl was motivated by the enthusiasm of the bank employees he met. He calls the experience his "five-year love-in." The volunteers represented every line of the bank's business and turned out to work with him in Idaho, Florida, Oregon, Texas, the District of Columbia, New York City, Dallas, Baltimore, cities across the Carolinas, and elsewhere. He arrived at work sites wearing worn jeans, scuffed work boots, and a stars-and-stripes bandana that he tied around his head to keep the sweat out of his eyes. A leather work belt cinched around his waist had pouch for a tape measure and pockets for nails. His favorite sixteen-ounce framing hammer was hung in a holster like one of his six-shooters he carries at his Texas ranch.

His favorite job, the one that inspires a lot of Habitat workers, was framing the walls and seeing them raised to give immediate shape and definition to a new home. He worked anywhere he was asked to, however. A reporter in a Virginia suburb of Washington, D.C., found him on top of a ladder, nails clinched in his teeth, as he hammered away to finish a closet. McColl told a reporter in Memphis that he really enjoyed the physical labor: "You can make a lot of money managing an office, but it's not the same as actually doing something with your hands." (On this trip, work continued through a rainstorm and McColl slipped and nearly fell from a second story.)

To him, the experience went beyond simply accomplishing a task and seeing the results. "You've made a difference in the lives of a family," he told a Charlotte newspaper reporter. "I think the people who have the ability, either physical or financial, should use it to help other people. I don't know of a better way to do that than helping to build someone a house."

In some locations, crews busied themselves with more than just houses. In Memphis, McColl's team helped build a house in Porter-Leath neighborhood, while other bank volunteers refurbished a playground and the grounds of a youth center. One weekend McColl left a Habitat build in St. Louis for a plane ride to Wichita Falls, Texas, where he participated in a 5K run to raise money for a local charity. Then, he went out to the Habitat work site.

Over the course of the bank's five-year project, some 20,000 people from Bank of America offices participated in Habitat builds. Not all of them swung a hammer with the man himself, but most did. The work projects became popular up and down the ranks. Bank executives in Texas used slots on the building team to reward high performers, who were flown to work sites where they spent a couple of days working side by side with the crew from Charlotte. Because they had done just about every job, McColl's teammates often served as construction leaders.

McColl, in his signature red, white, and blue bandana, worked from coast to coast. (Photo courtesy of Juan Lozano)

McColl brought the star power, but he worked just as hard, banged as many fingers, and produced as much sweat as everyone else. Those who followed him on these trips believed they were among the privileged. Juan Lozano reviewed the bank's regulatory filings for a living; he built Habitat houses for fun. Among his trips with McColl was one to LaGrange, Georgia, on a Jimmy Carter work project, an annual build designed to raise cash and visibility for the organization. Lozano was tuned in to his own task but was working close enough to the former president and his wife to hear Rosalynn remind her husband not to forget to go over and speak to

McColl. "I mean, this guy was the president of the United States," Lozano says, "and [Carter's] wife is prodding him to go say hello to Hugh McColl. It was far beyond anything I have ever seen before or will ever see again."

David Walker retired in 2019 after thirty years with the bank. He accompanied McColl on nearly twenty building trips, including one in Mexico where the heat and humidity were oppressive and the only shade on the building site was a small pop-up tent. One day, he looked over and saw McColl with his shirt off, his torso drenched in sweat. "Here is a guy who is retired. He is very wealthy," Walker said. "He could be anywhere in the world he wanted to be, doing anything in the world that he wanted to do, and this is what he chose to do."

McColl's crew played as hard as it worked. Some of the Charlotte regulars called themselves the BBC team, or the Build and Brew Crew, in honor of Lozano, who introduced his mates to craft beers, replacing what he called the "yellow, fizzy water" in the plane's cooler. After a weeklong build in Mexico, the crew's margarita tab cost more than their rooms—in a town where liquor was cheaper than water. On trips out Texas way, McColl rewarded the team with overnight stops at his ranch. There they enjoyed thick steaks, good whiskey, and evenings of "Texas TV," McColl's term for conversation enjoyed around the fireplace.

Getting to know homeowners wasn't possible everywhere, but it was part of the experience, especially on the lengthy tours in Mexico, where the work went on for five days. In these Mexican villages, Lozano said, children hadn't seen many people from the States, but they gravitated to the gray-haired gringo who was closer to their size and greeted them with a big toothy grin. They called him "abuelo," or grandfather, as they climbed on his back or rolled him around in a wheelbarrow.

Still vivid in McColl's mind, a decade or more later, was a woman who lived with her son and daughter in a hovel. It was the only shelter they could find after fleeing an abusive husband and father. "It was a stick house," McColl said. "I mean, out of sticks tied together. The woman had a little bit of tin or plastic on top. The floor was dirt. We built her a house that had a bathroom, a kitchen, and a bedroom and a living room. Everybody that went on that trip ended up in tears." While he and his crew were in town looking for a watering hole with a television tuned to

Panthers football, McColl noticed a kitchen set in a store window. He bought it and had it delivered to the woman's house. Later, McColl told Suits, "She has nothing in her current home. Every family needs a dining room table to sit around and join together."

On June 18, 2004, he celebrated his sixty-ninth birthday along with five hundred volunteers from the city's banks. That day they'd completed an extraordinary one-day build, a five-bedroom, 1,400-square-foot house for Jannie Grier and her five grandchildren. That house in west Charlotte's Oakview Terrace neighborhood marked McColl's forty-eighth build since 2002 in Washington Heights. Over cake, the huge crew serenaded him with a chorus of "Happy Birthday."

In July 2006, the McColl Habitat project's one hundredth house in the United States was in Charlotte's Druid Hills neighborhood. The number rose to 110 in August. In October, McColl was back in Texas, at Midland, where he and a crew spent three days working on three houses with about a hundred volunteers and the top echelon of Bank of America's management.

Bank of America's Habitat project included building teams in Mexico where McColl and his crew spent more than a week working daily with community volunteers. The neighborhood children in Puerto Escondido gravitated to McColl, whom they called their "abuelo." (Photo courtesy of Juan Lozano)

The work came to an end in 2007, with 123 homes built in communities from Oregon to southern Florida. Another one hundred homes were built in Mexico and farther south in Latin America. The Bank of America expanded the original gift to Habitat for a total of $16 million. McColl wasn't particularly ready to stop, but everything was upended as the nation's financial system went into free fall in 2008.

For McColl, the Habitat project extended relationships with his partners and teammates at the bank, cherished beyond the day when they—and he—would have become just a memory. He thrived on the challenge and the possibilities that arose on each outing, continuing a bond with old colleagues like Brenda Suits, and meeting new people where otherwise he was just a name. When it was over, he had people who jumped at the chance to ride with him again.

He has continued to scratch his Habitat itch as a member of a Covenant Presbyterian Church building team. They work in the back reaches of the mountains in Avery County, North Carolina. While most Charlotteans know the area around Linville, Banner Elk, and Newland for the golf courses and large resort-style homes that sit atop the mountains or overlook plush fairways, McColl and Bob Henderson, Covenant's senior pastor, have a different appreciation for the area. Work teams head there yearly. McColl's been something of a regular.

McColl was over seventy years old when he began working with Henderson, who marveled at his friend's energy and resourcefulness. McColl no longer tried to heft fifty-pound bags of concrete, but he could still manage a hammer. One day Henderson spotted McColl, trying to work a stubborn rafter into place, pull out his phone and make a call. Henderson was close enough to hear him say, "Hey, I'm looking at this joint, and it has got this angle." It finally dawned on Henderson that McColl was phoning for advice. "He is consulting some guy, who knows where, to solve this construction problem. The fact that Hugh McColl, thirteen years into retirement, had a Habitat construction crew supervisor's number on his phone is telling."

Henderson continued: "We were driving down Highway 221 in Avery County, exhausted after working on houses for about three days, having long days, and he said, 'You know, you guys don't believe in breaks, do you?' We had put in sixteen-hour days. This was early in my relationship with him, and he said, 'I can see how you're making a difference here. You're making a difference.'" Henderson said McColl paused and looked over and added, "At my funeral, I want you to say, 'He tried to make a difference.'"

"Well, Hugh," Henderson responded, "I think it's pretty clear that you've made a difference. Why don't I just talk about the difference you've made?"

"No," he said, "say I tried."

Chapter Three
Doing Business

Though Hugh McColl officially stepped down as CEO and chairman of Bank of America April 25, 2001, he left the job a bit earlier to spend a couple weeks at his Texas ranch. There, unmolested by the outside world, he could begin to reboot his life. McColl had a list of topics he wanted to learn more about during his "Chapter Two." He planned to travel with his wife, Jane, build more Habitat houses, enjoy time with his grandchildren, and spend more time at the ranch. He also contemplated a proposition made by a younger associate at the bank.

In his absence, Pat Hinson, who had left the bank with her boss, outfitted a new office for McColl, one provided as part of his retirement package. On prominent display, centered on a small conference table, was the outsized crystal grenade. Family photos and an array of mementoes were on view, along with stock certificates bearing the McColl name, displayed sequentially, from American Trust Company, founded early in the twentieth century, through North Carolina National Bank, and on to the twenty-first century, capturing the chain of mergers that ended with Bank of America.

Two large paintings occupied prominent positions. One, a favorite McColl picked up in South Africa, depicts a sweeping landscape backed by the tall peaks of the Drakensburg Range. Large, billowing clouds, rising from the Indian Ocean on the eastern slopes, are set against a dazzling blue sky. Flanking it is *Take the Money and Run*, by Phoenix artist Dan Mieduch. McColl commissioned the painting after seeing Mieduch's bank robbery painting, *The Lord Helps*, in a Dallas gallery. The commissioned work features three bandits, smothered in smoke from their six-guns as they shoot their way out of town. Loose currency flutters to the ground and horses kick up plenty of dust as the bandits make their getaway. The smoke and dust, however, don't obscure the name on the bank they robbed: Republic Bank, i.e., McColl's favorite Dallas bank, the one NCNB took over in 1988 with the help of the federal government. "That's the bank that made us all rich," he says.

A few weeks into retirement and back in Charlotte, McColl discovered that the telephone didn't ring like it used to. He had a fine office in the Bank of America Corporate Center, fifty-one stories above the city, but nothing was happening. The telephone was silent.

One day Jane got a call from Hugh offering to help her complete some routine errands. He asked where she was. What was she doing? Jane said, "I thought, 'This is not going to work if he's going to keep tracking me down going to the dry cleaners.'"

As the silence grew heavier, McColl called David Vorhoff.

Unsure where his plans might take him, Vorhoff had phoned McColl's office asking for a few minutes of his time a few months before McColl's retirement date. He awkwardly delivered an abbreviated version of a post-retirement proposition to McColl's gatekeeper and figured that might easily be the end of it. To his surprise, thirty minutes later he had a meeting with the chairman.

Vorhoff had built his career at the bank, starting his service with NCNB more than a dozen years earlier before it scooped up First Republic Bank in Texas. Now he was a managing director in Banc of America Securities, handling mergers and acquisitions in the health care sector.

Vorhoff had first discussed his proposition with Eric Andreozzi, a merger and acquisitions guy at First Union Securities. Over lunch, the two friends had talked about the potential for a small firm, based in Charlotte, that would focus on finding buyers for family-owned businesses and middle-market enterprises valued at less than $250 million. The size cap meant they could easily accommodate clients that Bank of

America, just like Merrill Lynch, would find too small to be worth their while.

Vorhoff couldn't have landed on a more appealing proposal for McColl. It checked virtually all the boxes for a man of his corporate stature. The man's desk was already stacked with offers: directorships at high-profile companies, alliances with financial houses, lots of money, lots of prestige, and usually not a lot of work. Mostly, those seeking his attention wanted a name for their letterheads. None of that interested McColl.

Vorhoff was offering McColl a chance to stay right where he wanted to be, in Charlotte, North Carolina, working in the trenches with people he already knew. With the cap on client size, there would be no conflicts with the bank, and the offer contained something other corporate arrangements could not—unfettered freedom, especially from financial industry regulators.

McColl didn't accept Vorhoff's offer immediately. He let it perk and asked his son, Hugh III, to weigh in on the seventeen-page business plan. Recognizing his own propensity to believe anything was possible—he is a glass-half-full kind of guy—he was sure his son's more critical review would reveal the downside. When it didn't, and McColl was satisfied he had something he could work with, he phoned Vorhoff and McColl Partners was launched. (The firm name was a bit of a misnomer; McColl was not a partner in McColl Partners. Rather, he owned a majority interest in the McColl Group, the company that owned McColl Partners.)

It took some time for the particulars to come together, but on September 10, 2001, the day before Islamic terrorists flew hijacked airliners in to New York's Twin Towers, McColl and Vorhoff received final approval from federal regulators that permitted their investment banking firm, McColl Partners, to begin accepting clients.

McColl and others on the original staff were preparing to move into their new offices in the Bank of America Corporate Center just as the planes turned and headed toward Wall Street. No one had settled in as the news of the attack broke and the wall-to-wall television coverage began. McColl and Vorhoff watched it unfold on a screen in the conference room. When they looked out the window to the southwest, they could see airliners that had been ordered out of the sky making enforced and unscheduled landings at Douglas International. McColl got word that their building was being evacuated due to concern that the bank tower might be a terrorist target. All the offices emptied, as did others in high rise buildings along Tryon Street. Twenty-eight thousand people hurried away from the center of the city.

A month later, when the principals of McColl Partners arrived in New York to introduce their firm to Wall Street, Lower Manhattan still smelled of destruction. Laying the groundwork for their new company's future, McColl had arranged a visit with Merrill Lynch's Thundering Herd to let them know that McColl Partners was ready to take on any clients Merrill found too small.

A dozen years later, when McColl Partners was sold to Deloitte Corporate Finance, the firm was handling more of Merrill's referrals than any of its competitors.

At the outset, before there were any clients or fees to be had, McColl set the table for the firm's operations. McColl's name guaranteed an entrée to corporate suites all around the world. Virtually no one in American business was likely to refuse to take his call. However, until McColl Partners began generating income, he personally paid the employees' salaries. That trip to New York, as well as other travel, was charged against McColl's annual credit of 150 hours of private jet service, which was, along with his office space, part of his retirement package from Bank of America.

As McColl remembers those early days: "It gave me a transition from having nothing to do, literally, to having something that I could be active in. I could open any door anywhere. So they were riding on my access. The transactions didn't interest me particularly, but it was action that I liked."

McColl Partners proved to be the best choice McColl could have made when he stepped back from running Bank of America. The work certainly played to his strengths. He had been making deals since his salad days in the 1960s, when NCNB was just an up-and-comer. His negotiating skill, even then, was notable. He once helped his boss, Addison Reese, negotiate to buy a small-town bank only to be told just hours later to go back and kill the deal. Then, forty-eight hours after that, with the seller still bewildered, McColl was ordered to reboot the arrangements without telling the buyer of the confusion at NCNB. McColl pulled it off, and everyone went home happy. In the years that followed he really had no match for the hundreds of acquisitions that turned NCNB into NationsBank and then Bank of America, the nation's first coast-to-coast retail banking franchise.

McColl Partners not only suited his temperament and his ambitions, it also made him an awful lot of money, much of which he subsequently channeled into various philanthropies. As far as he was concerned, the only downside was reading newspaper accounts that identified him as an "investment banker." Throughout his career McColl had considered investment bankers a disagreeable and greedy lot whose only allegiance was to money. Vorhoff summed up the irony. "One of the definitions of an investment banker is a deal maker. Look at what he did. He was one of the greatest investment bankers that ever lived, but he didn't want to be called an investment banker."

Vorhoff and Andreozzi were the managing directors at McColl Partners. Joining Andreozzi from First Union were Philip Colaco and Lorin DeMordant, who came aboard as vice presidents. Jamie Lewin and Bradley Winer came in as associates. Most of the others came out of the old Bowles Hollowell Conner firm, whose founder, Erskine Bowles, had received a boost from McColl twenty-plus years earlier when he was setting up his first investment banking business.

McColl's joint ownership of the firm meant he did not have to register with regulators, a relief after a lifetime of working in a regulated environment. It didn't preclude him from bringing clients to the table, many of whom he knew well. For example, Cameron M. "Cammie" Harris of Charlotte became a client when he set out to sell his insurance agency, a multistate moneymaker with about 230 employees. Harris's father had been on the NCNB board when it was organized in 1960, and McColl had helped the elder Harris's sons, including Cammie, clear financial hurdles through the years. In the early aughts, Cameron M. Harris & Co. was headed toward becoming a part of BB&T when McColl reminded Harris of their long association. After talking with Wachovia CEO, Ken Thompson, McColl brought Harris a substitute deal with a $30 million premium—160 percent more than what BB&T was going to pay.

When Raleigh businessman Temple Sloan got ready to sell one of his companies, he didn't forget the man who had put him on the NationsBank board of directors in 1996 and carried him forward as a director at Bank of America. The two had come to know one another well. They had hunted together at McColl's place in Texas, and

McColl had spent time at Sloan's own vast ranch on Montana's western border. Sloan once snapped a photograph of McColl branding calves. Sloan's sale of his ready-mix concrete business in 2003 turned out to be a joint effort with another firm that included Glenn Orr, the former BB&T president. McColl Partners picked up its fee from the $210 million sale and then went on to arrange a dozen more as the ready-mix concrete business went through a period of consolidation. The commissions earned from the sale of Sloan's company were compounded from one transaction to the next.

McColl was a regular presence in the firm's offices on the fifty-first floor, where his own private office was located. When he wasn't downtown, he was as close as his cell phone. While he had spent most of his career on the buy side, he was comfortable selling, too, and was especially effective when the occasion called for his gravitas. Having been down that road many times, he had an instinct for knowing when customers needed the calming influence of gray hair and experience.

Looking back, Vorhoff says those years spent with Hugh McColl were the most transformative of his life. Nothing could compare. McColl told him at the outset, "You know I spent my entire career building a reputation, and it only takes one bad deal to ruin it." That became a litmus test. Potential clients who came in the door boosting sketchy transactions were advised to go elsewhere. "We were extremely sensitive to our senior partner whose name was on the door," Vorhoff said. "It kept us on the straight and narrow."

Often, what corporate CEOs miss most when they leave office are the power and the perks. For McColl, it was the people. At his elbow when he retired was a team that had been with him for decades. He had shared with these men and women his greatest successes and his most frightening moments, such as a fiery forced landing of NationsBank's big G4 at Dulles International in 1997. McColl knew that he was always better at what he did when he had his people around him. He could feel the energy they transmitted. That was corporate speak, but also a sincere description founded in a sense of loyalty and personal commitment that went both ways.

None had known him longer that Pat Hinson. When she decided to retire a few years into the era of McColl Partners, McColl despaired ever finding a suitable replacement. Their minds had worked like one for so long that he told his wife he could say "get that son of a bitch on the phone" and Pat would know which son of a bitch he was talking about. "I had left a family at the bank," McColl said one day as he looked back on his retirement. "It was a huge family that I was really tight with and enjoyed being with."

At McColl Partners, he developed an especially strong bond with those on the firm's ground floor, the analysts working in the interior cubicles, some of whom still had strains of "Pomp and Circumstance" ringing in their ears. They exchanged college life for eighty-hour workweeks in what amounted to a boot camp for financial tycoons and hedge fund managers. The expectation for these young recruits was to put in two years of hard labor before moving on to graduate school or earning a slot in the next level of the financial industry. McColl Partners appealed to these newbies for the same reason clients were attracted to the firm—a chance to work with Hugh McColl. And the firm delivered; there was no middle management at McColl Partners.

"He can connect with everybody, whether it's a cab driver or a corporate type."

—SCOTT WERRY

In the bullpen in the summer of 2003 were David Sheffer and Scott Werry. David excelled in business school and Scott was a Morehead-Cain scholar. To Scott Werry, McColl was just a name on a building at the Kenan-Flagler Business School when the man himself stopped to shake Werry's hand. Werry was finishing up a dance marathon at the Carolina Inn to raise money for the North Carolina Children's Hospital; McColl was leaving a meeting of the UNC–CH board of trustees.

Werry was raised on a dairy farm an hour east of Toronto, Canada. Seventeen years after he began his tenure at McColl Partners, he still looked like a twenty-something youth pastor. The inexpensive Timex watch on his wrist did nothing to suggest he was the founder and leading principal at a $7 billion private equity fund, or a man, who along with Sheffer, handled the $2.7 billion sale of a controlling interest in MyEyeDr.com, a group of more than 500 eye-care practices that Sheffer had invested in and organized from thirty-five practices seven years earlier.

Putting together deals is just a small slice of Werry's memory of his two years at McColl Partners. Much more vivid are recollections of the one-on-one time with the man himself. Their interactions often took place over lunch at the kind of diners that sell fish tacos or serve vegetables family-style. McColl loves spots like that, and taking his teammates to lunch there was his way of breaking them out of their Uptown Charlotte bubble.

"He'd just swing by the cube and say to all the analysts, 'Let's go grab lunch,'" recalled Werry. No one begged off. Phone calls abruptly ended. Computer screens went dark. One day the group ended up at a greasy spoon on Charlotte's south side where the waiter made a point of thanking McColl for what he had done for Charlotte. "I was twenty-three and thinking, 'Here we are, really far from Uptown and really far from the front page of *The Wall Street Journal*, and here we've got someone who recognizes him and is thanking him for all he's done.' That was pretty neat."

"I learned more in those lunches than I ever did in the classroom," Werry continued. "He talked to us about leadership and building organizations, but he also coached us on economics, politics, community engagement, and even how to propose to your wife and how to think about raising a family or being a father."

Werry watched and listened. "He'd call on clients, and one of the gifts he has is he can connect with everybody, whether it's a cab driver or a corporate type. He has such a sincere interest in people. He taught us to really take time to get to know everybody, not just the folks in the corporate tower."

David Sheffer, founder of MyEyeDr.com (his father is an optometrist), grew up in Charlotte. Once he heard of McColl's plans for a M&A firm, he badgered the recruiter at McColl Partners until he got an interview. Sheffer had spent the summer of 2002 as an intern at JPMorgan Chase and Company and had an offer for a slot in New York when he accepted a job at McColl Partners, a year-old firm with a staff of ten. "I was willing to go against the grain, go work for a startup firm, go live in Charlotte, all to really be associated with him, just by association, much less actually work with him."

Like Werry, Sheffer absorbed lessons in personal values as well as politics. "He showed me very quickly that you can be a white, wealthy southerner and a Democrat." He said McColl taught him how to remain consistent and steady in his convictions even in the face of a contrary political environment.

McColl Partners was a generalist firm. One day analysts were researching the restaurant business and another tracking the future of companies producing ready-mixed concrete. It was their job to gather the financial data on a client's business and its market so the partners could sound knowledgeable in that crucial first meeting. Sheffer marveled at McColl's capacity to absorb details and found him a relentless note taker who admonished the younger men to always have a pen handy. That probably wasn't in the JPMorgan training manual. Neither were the periodic tests of the ten frequently misused and misspelled words that McColl was given to administering.

Sheffer, inspired by McColl's altruism, joined him on a few of the monthly Habitat for Humanity trips, including one where McColl routed the bank's plane to Georgia to pick up Habitat founder Millard Fuller. "I didn't know what I was getting into. I just knew I wanted to be around him," he said. "Those builds were some of my favorite memories because he

> "Everybody's wealthy and everybody's powerful and yet they have no power at Augusta."
> —HUGH McCOLL

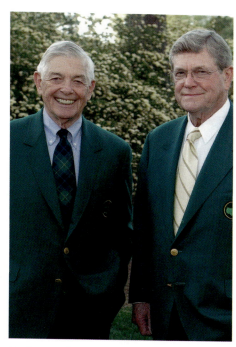

Hugh McColl joined the Augusta National Golf Club in the mid-1970s and was close to the club leadership from the outset. He served as club treasurer under a succession of chairmen beginning with the late Hootie Johnson, pictured here with McColl in their distinctive green blazers. A leading South Carolina banker, Johnson once tried to hire a young McColl away from North Carolina National Bank. (Photo courtesy of Hugh McColl Jr.)

just got right in the mix."

Sheffer was working his usual hours—which meant he didn't leave the office before midnight—when McColl showed up at around two a.m. one Wednesday morning after an extended absence from Charlotte. He stopped in to sort through his mail and was surprised to find Sheffer still at work. When Sheffer explained his late hours were routine, McColl said, "Well, grab two people and meet me at the private air hangar on Thursday at eight a.m. We're going to play golf at Augusta."

"It was just out of left field," Sheffer remembers. "He didn't know if I played golf. He didn't know who I'd bring. He just thought I was working too hard."

Sheffer invited his father and uncle to round out the foursome and was surprised when the club's chairman, Billy Payne, personally welcomed them to the course. After a day on the course and dinner at the club, they returned to Charlotte. (Sheffer bade his relatives good night and headed to the office to catch up.)

McColl joined Augusta National Golf Club in 1975, the final year that Clifford Roberts, the club's founder, was in command. McColl's two sponsors could not have been more influential. One was South Carolina banker Hootie Johnson, who would later chair the executive committee at both NationsBank and Bank of America, and Jack Stephens, a Little Rock, Arkansas, oil and gas billionaire, whose cabin at Augusta is two doors from the Eisenhower Cabin. Johnson and Stephens later chaired the club's board and oversaw the annual premier golf event, the Masters Tournament.

Though Roberts took a shine to him, McColl found the man to be imperious and prickly. Nonetheless, whenever Roberts drafted him for a foursome he accepted. To McColl's chagrin, golfing with Roberts consumed an entire day. He didn't tee off until ten a.m., and after nine holes they broke for lunch. "It was all a gentleman's game with him and not to be rushed," McColl remembered. "I would get to jumping out of my skin. I like to walk up to the ball, hit it, and keep moving. But I played with him a lot, so I became involved with the top of the club because of those friendships."

McColl became close to Stephens, Augusta's chairman throughout the 1990s. He served on the executive committee with Stephens's successors, Hootie Johnson (1998–2006), Billy Payne of Atlanta (2006–2017), and Fred S. Ridley, the Tampa lawyer and U.S. amateur champion who followed Payne. As chair of the club's finance committee, McColl submitted an annual financial report that was conclusive and succinct, in the Roberts tradition. "Well, we paid all our bills," McColl said when called upon by the chair, "and the stuff we don't talk about, we've got a hell of a lot more of it." There were never any questions. "It's run well," McColl said. "You are supposed to go have a good time and not worry about the details."

Tenure and connections are the currency at Augusta. "Everything down there is according to a pecking order. You don't get told where you are in the pecking order, but you can tell by the room you get," McColl said. "I always get a good room." During the club's winter-to-spring season, McColl may not play golf but once or twice. "It is one of the anomalies, of all the anomalies, that I have this position of influence in a sport that I am not really that good at."

McColl turns out for the Masters Tournament in April, dons his green blazer, and circulates among the club's membership of about three hundred. After decades of being in, or close to, the club's leadership, he stepped down from the executive committee at the conclusion of the 2019 season and carried home a painting of the clubhouse and a plaque made of wood from the Eisenhower Tree, a tall loblolly pine. The tree was cut down after sustaining damage from a 2014 ice storm, sixty years after Dwight Eisenhower had first lobbied to have it removed, complaining that it obstructed his shots off the seventeenth tee. There are seedlings in the nursery that will replace the loblolly, in the same spot, once one is hardy enough to be set out.

Some things just don't change at Augusta. It is, and has been since it opened in 1932, one of the most exclusive clubs in the country, a haven for the nation's corporate elite. For example, one day McColl ended up in a foursome with investment genius Warren Buffet, Microsoft founder Bill Gates, and real estate mogul Tom Cousins of Atlanta. It's run by its own traditions, most of which are simply understood. "Everybody's wealthy and everybody's powerful, and yet they have no power at Augusta," McColl said. "The chairman runs everything. You have a dictatorship. So when something works, you don't screw with it."

For years all-white and all-male, the club now has at least six women members and a handful of nonwhites. McColl sponsored the club's second African American member in the early 1990s at the same time that he was working to diversify membership at Charlotte's country clubs.

McColl's credentials at Augusta have long been one of his most valuable assets though his own father consistently resisted the club's allure. For thirty years, until his death in his eighties, the elder McColl golfed daily at the Marlboro Country Club. He played a round with whomever was available, had a beer, and then went home. He repeatedly turned down invitations to meet his son at Augusta.

David Vorhoff, not knowing how to play the game, consistently declined McColl's offers as well. Privately, he took pleasure in being a golf agnostic. Finally, his wife, Erin, in a conspiracy with McColl, presented him with a package of six lessons. Vorhoff completed the lessons and felt bound to accept McColl's next invitation. Vorhoff made it through eighteen holes, shooting par on at least one. He enjoyed a memo-

> McColl considered himself the luckiest man alive.

Hugh McColl finished his training as a Marine Corps officer in the mid-1950s but it took sixty years for the U.S. Department of Veterans Affairs to approve coverage of the GI Bill as a veteran of the conflict in Lebanon. At age eighty-five, he was considering taking advantage of his new college tuition benefits. In the early aughts, McColl revisited his last duty station in Puerto Rico on a pleasure outing accompanied by a group of young analysts from McColl Partners. (Photo courtesy of Hugh McColl Jr.)

rable dinner at the clubhouse, where Jeff Immelt, the CEO at GE, his board members in tow, warmly greeted McColl. After that one round, however, Vorhoff gave away his clubs, making him perhaps the only person in the world to have played his first and last round—his *only* round—of golf at Augusta National.

Vorhoff says McColl's commitment to the youngest members of the firm was extraordinary. Once a year, McColl took the most junior staff on a trip of their choosing. They would be gone three or four days, traveling in the boss's plane to Las Vegas or an exotic spot like the Atlantis resort in the Bahamas. One year, McColl persuaded them to join him in Puerto Rico for a visit to the island of Vieques, where he had participated in Marine Corps amphibious training. He wanted one more assault on Red Beach. The dates of the outing coincided with San Juan Day, when local tradition required beachside bonfires and jumping fully clothed and backward into the ocean at midnight for a year's worth of cleansing, purification, and good luck. McColl considered himself the luckiest man alive.

"I would argue Hugh's greatest impact at the end of the day might have been on the lives of the young analysts that we hired," Vorhoff said. "He took real energy from the youth and the passion, the young men and women, and he loved mentoring them, he loved helping them." This extra attention had some of the firm's vice presidents wishing they had been able to join the company earlier in their careers.

When Sheffer began making plans to leave McColl Partners, he stopped by the founder's office to tell him that he was lining up interviews. "What are your top five firms or the top cities where you want to live?" McColl asked. Sheffer rattled off his list, and McColl began making calls to the heads of the firms where Sheffer had an interest. These are places where it's hard to get an interview, much less a job, and Sheffer was hearing McColl on the phone saying, "Lou, it's Hugh, I've got a good man that I really think highly of." As McColl handed the contact off to Sheffer, McColl dialed again and again, lining up interviews. "Within two minutes of telling him I'm leaving the firm he founded, he's helping me get my next job," Sheffer remembers. "Who does that?"

Others left Charlotte with handwritten letters of introduction to the Harvard Business School and, in some cases, an endorsement from McColl's friend C. D.

Spangler, one of Harvard's favorite alumni and a member of the school's board of overseers. There was talk that some of the larger investment houses complained to the school that a higher percentage of McColl Partners analysts were winning admission at Harvard than those from Wall Street outfits like Goldman Sachs.

McColl Partners had yet to close its first deal when McColl's name showed up on another new firm, McColl Garella. It was decidedly different. His partner was Julie Garella, who had ambitions of extending merger and acquisition services to women-owned businesses.

In the summer of 2001, Garella argued her place into the all-male space of McColl Partners. Garella had recently turned forty and was leaving a small private equity firm she had organized when she pitched McColl on backing her as the firm's specialist on women-owned businesses. She volunteered to work on commission only, or, as she put it, "eat-what-I-kill." The introduction to her soon-to-be colleagues came a day or so before 9/11, when she was shown the firm's space on the fifty-first floor. Each office she passed had long-distance views—except hers. It was a windowless room next to the copy machine. She didn't complain; Garella was happy to be on the roster. When she reported to work a few days later, however, she had been reassigned to more agreeable quarters on the other end of the floor in an office with a window. No one said a word, but she knew who had made it happen.

"I think when I threw the idea at him, it wasn't a stretch for him to see that was an underserved part of the investment banking business," Garella recalled more than a decade later. In the intervening years, she has written a primer on raising money for startups. "It might be hard to imagine that now, but then it was a rarity, especially in Charlotte, North Carolina."

Using her own network of women entrepreneurs, Garella brought in the firm's first client, although it didn't really fit the women-owned definition. This initial success didn't ease the tension with her colleagues, and it was apparent that a different arrangement might be in order. That was when McColl and Garella arrived at the idea of creating a separate firm. These days McColl says, "My partners didn't like her; they didn't think she was qualified." Garella says the arrangement worked as well as it could have, considering the times. "I think we moved the needle a little bit."

The business appealed to McColl's record of expanding opportunities for women, something he had begun devoting attention to in the mid- and late-1980s, well before most corporations began paying attention to retaining and cultivating talented women in their ranks. Under his command, NCNB introduced flexible work schedules to accommodate working mothers and provided childcare subsidies for salaried employees. He built a first-class childcare center within sight of the bank's headquarters as part of the overhaul of downtown Charlotte. The bank also eliminated rules that stripped women of tenure and retirement credits should they leave their jobs to have children. Paid maternity and paternity leave for new parents became a standard benefit.

Karen Geiger served as McColl's point person on raising the status of women and helped shape his strategies. An unrestrained New Jersey native, she was a new employee in 1982 when she met McColl in the elevator. She had finished telling an off-color joke when he introduced himself and asked her name. Nearly forty years later, she remembers thinking: "This is my last day here." On the contrary, when the two worked together on human resources issues related to work and family, McColl came to appreciate Geiger's willingness to speak her mind. He tasked her with implementing changes that began to reverse institutional bias against women. Later, McColl charged Geiger with identifying women who possessed the talent and capacity for executive positions.

An early change involved the rule prohibiting married couples from working at the bank. If coworkers married, one partner had to leave, and that often was the woman. Forcing talented people, many of whom his bank had trained, to leave didn't make sense to McColl, especially when many of those went on to take jobs with the competition.

Even when Geiger was sidelined with injuries after Hurricane Hugo brought a tree down on her house, McColl sought her counsel. He would drop in for bedside visits with little or no notice, bringing questions about troubling management issues. She returned to work and later earned a doctorate in leadership and change.

Geiger didn't play golf so her boss hadn't had the same kind of opportunities to get to know her as he enjoyed with his male employees. She volunteered that her favorite pastime was Wednesday night movie outings with her husband. Two weeks later McColl called and asked if he and Jane could meet the Geigers at the theater. That week, they were going to see *9 to 5*, a comedy about three women who kidnap their insensitive boss. "Oh my God! I was mortified," Geiger said. "That's the movie we went to. Afterwards we went out for a drink. That's how you get to know me. It was pretty cool. I didn't have to change my lifestyle to become known."

McColl recognized early on that improving working conditions for women was a business issue that came with social benefits. "He wanted to buy banks," Geiger said, "and this softened his image, because he was seen as a tough Marine, which he's not. But that's the view of him. Out there on the family-friendly front, he could get a different reputation." McColl and NCNB ended up on the cover of *Working Women*, which annually highlighted female-friendly workplaces in America. There was no mention of hand grenades or lessons from the Marine Corps. The bank's progressive record was not only female friendly but family friendly. It gave McColl talking points for years to come.

Bold moves like establishing McColl Garella kept Charlotte's most popular corporate retiree in public view. People wanted to know what he thought about civic affairs, he was asked to comment on the state of American business, and readers followed his passion for art, the Charlotte Symphony, and even the happenings in Texas, where his ranch hands sculpted large chunks of mesquite into blocky end tables that sold for $900 in Erin Vorhoff's shop, with the profits shared by those who made them. A *Charlotte Observer* columnist said McColl was Charlotte's answer to Lorenzo de Medici, the fifteenth-century Italian patron of culture, the arts, and statecraft.

One spring weekend in 2003, about 150 CEOs, educators, economists, writers, and activists came together at Charlotte's Ballantyne Resort to consider the moral dimensions of business. The sizable crowd was attributed largely to McColl's name on the invitation, but was also due in part because McColl lined up his friend Warren Buffett as a keynote speaker. Certainly, the environment was ripe for some reflection. The markets had been rocked by the collapse of the dot-com companies, and prosecutors were still unwinding the scandal at Enron, a national energy company that failed and took with it the accounting firm Arthur Anderson. The collapse of WorldCom, a communications company, produced the largest bankruptcy filing in history. The country had soured over the state of corporate responsibility.

The conference was the product of conversations between two Charlotteans: securities consultant Chris William, the host of *Carolina Business Review*, a weekly program on public television, and event planner Mary Tribble. William talked weekly with CEOs and often touched on questions of ethics, values, and corporate leadership. Sloshing through that topic with Tribble, who had clients wrestling with the same issues, the two began an extended session by CEOs on corporate sustainability, or how companies can be profitable and help society and the environment at the same time. They took the idea to McColl; he signed on immediately. "It's the right topic at the right time and the right audience," McColl told them. He put in his call to Buffett.

The program came together over a period of months, and it was ready to go just as the Ballantyne, a luxury hotel south of Charlotte, was opening for general use. Buffett kicked off things Friday evening with a blunt assessment of the whopping pay gap between corporate executives and the people who work for them. He said it was time for corporate leaders to regain the trust of the public. Economist Jeremy Rifkin gave a talk promoting the benefits of hydrogen fuel cells; a former CEO of Royal Dutch/Shell, the multinational oil company, also gave a presentation; and multiple small-group sessions focused on social and environmental issues. McColl led a conversation on low-income schools. Writer Tom Wolfe, whose book, *The Bonfire of the Vanities*, centered on corporate greed, was the closing speaker on Sunday. As the weekend came to an end, Ernesto Cortes from Industrial Areas Foundation, the spawn of social activist Saul Alinsky, asked whether the corporate leaders, now awakened to community needs, "were willing to bridge the gap between the cup and the lip."

In 2004, Charlotte's Echo Foundation chose McColl for its annual award that recognizes those who have carried forward Nobel laureate Elie Wiesel's call for human dignity, justice, and moral courage. Past recipients include Harvard's Henry Louis

Gates Jr. and Dr. Bernard Kochner, the founder of Doctors Without Borders. Echo cited McColl "for championing universal access to economic opportunity and education as essential components of community development" and recognized his "many quiet acts of dignity, generosity and compassion."

Jane McColl received the award on behalf of her husband who was home recuperating. To the crowd, she joked about her husband's condition, but in private, she was less glib. There were times when his tendency to push to the limit gave her pause.

Before the foundation award was announced, McColl, during a pickup basketball game, injured his shoulder and left bicep and required surgery. He was still recovering from that when, in January 2005, he landed on the operating table again. Surgeons performed six bypasses on blocked arteries, with additional procedures for a total of six operations. The experience knocked him back like nothing he'd experienced before. He left the hospital weak, but resolved to rebuild his strength. His began an indoor regimen with a therapist and then moved outside, taking daily walks through the neighborhood.

During those weeks of rehabilitation, Scott Werry became a frequent sidewalk companion. The two had become especially close after McColl had arranged private air service to carry the entire firm to Canada for Werry's father's funeral. "That was pretty meaningful to me," Werry said in 2019. "That was fifteen years ago, but people still talk about that back home. That was very supportive."

Werry would meet up with McColl after working until two or three in the morning. "At first, he could barely get down the driveway, but he knew every day exactly where he wanted to go, and it was measured. His recovery was so much quicker than what the doctors thought because he was so determined. We just got a little bit longer every day. He was so determined to follow the routine. For me, that was some of the best memories at McColl Partners; just the time with him to be able to go and walk in the morning."

McColl made some adjustments to his lifestyle. The multiple procedures exacerbated his diabetes such that diet alone could no longer keep it under control, forcing him to begin insulin injections. He gave up his single-malt Scotch whiskey for wine and ate fewer donuts and sandwiches. He began to live a more measured life.

Build, build, and build had been a mantra for more than forty years.

Now, he realized that once his strength was restored, he needed a different mantra.

McColl could stand to trim his responsibilities. In addition to McColl Partners, he had organized McColl Fine Art, where he had about $10 million invested in art. He had opened a sales gallery in Charlotte's Dilworth neighborhood. The building had housed a branch office of the U.S. Postal Service before McColl burnished the floors of pale pine to a high shine and arrayed pieces that he had acquired against crisp white walls. Prices went as high as six figures. He had another gallery in New York and an arrangement with partners there to acquire and sell pieces, some of which were valued at six figures or more.

The entire operation was an extension of a passion for art that he inherited from his mother. She was an accomplished artist who maintained a studio in a small building behind the family home in Bennettsville. Hugh and Jane's personal collection included pieces that reminded them of their travels abroad. Most of these hang in their home in Eastover.

At commencement in June 2005, McColl stepped down as chair of the trustees of Queens University, where the business school carried his name. A generous Florida donor—a banker whose institution was acquired by NCNB—facilitated a $4 million gift to the school to launch the graduate program. He insisted it be named for McColl. McColl had been a trustee since 1983 and was named chair in 1991.

He began winding down McColl Garella toward the end of 2005. The firm had never made money. In fact, over the years, expenses had outrun income by several million dollars. "I think we gave it a really good shot," McColl said when the *Charlotte Business Journal* called to ask about the closing of the firm. "The opportunities to make it go were just not deep enough." Garella left Charlotte for New York and a job at Citigroup.

The size and value of McColl Partners deals continued to grow, cementing its reputation as a part of the city's emergence as a regional powerhouse. From 2001, with a head count of seven, the company had grown in four years to a staff of forty. McColl Partners moved into larger quarters on the fifty-fourth floor, space vacated by Price Waterhouse, which left behind so much polished granite and mahogany trim it would have been too costly to redecorate. McColl Partners moved up and Falfurrias Capital Partners moved in.

In spring 2006, at the age of seventy-one, McColl announced he was forming a private equity firm with partner Marc A. Oken, most recently Bank of America's chief financial officer. Oken and McColl had spent hours talking about how the two could make the most of their combined talents. With Falfurrias Capital, the two aimed to raise between $85 and $100 million to invest in medium-sized companies. The company drew its name from a town of about 5,000 in the Southeastern toe of Texas, about an hour's drive north of McColl's ranch.

Oken, a beefy guy with a broad, open face, and a receding hairline, is a dozen years McColl's junior. A CPA, his thing is numbers. He is a careful investor and drills down to the smallest details of a balance sheet.

In the late 1980s, accounting firm Price Waterhouse assigned Oken to Charlotte to handle the NCNB account. Not long after, Oken joined the bank. He worked there when it made its first trans-Mississippi acquisition in Texas, and from there, Oken remained part of McColl's expansion machine that turned a mid-sized regional bank into one that reached coast to coast.

In addition to their experience at the bank, Oken and McColl shared records of military service—Oken flew Navy fighters in Vietnam. They had been hunting birds together in Texas for years on thousands of acres of leased land the two held separately and together. Their politics were poles apart, but in 2006 they had a common purpose. "He loves to win," said Oken, "and I hate to lose."

Private equity had been on McColl's agenda for some time. It was on his short list when McColl Partners was in its infancy, but he quieted such talk after it became clear that even an appearance of a conflict of interest would complicate both enterprises.

By 2005, McColl Partners was well established, with a growing reputation for solid work, and McColl was ready for something new. Raising oceans of cash to buy companies, then reorganize or squeeze out the fat and make them profitable and eligible for sale, was something he knew quite well. When he was doing it for the bank, he got his bonuses in stock. Now, with his firm, he would get a piece of the action.

While their new partnership certainly opened doors, it didn't always close the sale. Potential investors were looking for an honest-to-goodness track record. Falfurrias didn't have one. Both Oken and McColl were baffled that early prospects questioned their confidence in success. "Nobody thought we knew anything about private equity," McColl recalled. "I had spent most of my career behaving like an investment bank, or a private bank. We did some very aggressive lending. We had that reputation. We helped make a lot of people rich." Recalling the doubt he heard in those early calls, he said, "It's really amazing."

Oken knew it didn't matter how impressive your credentials are. "You're starting over again as far as credibility with institutional investors who give you no credit for what you've done in a previous life," he said. "You've actually had to have a fund and successfully invest, and you do it again, and by the time you get to the third fund, 'Oh, yeah, we remember you. How'd you do the past five or six years?' It's quite aggravating, actually." The two responded by hiring thirty-year-old Ed McMahan whose resume included experience with private equity firms in Chicago and structuring transactions. McMahan made sure the trains ran on time and eventually took a lead in the firm.

The personal investments of McColl and Oken, a $20 million stake from Bank of America, and another $15 million from Wachovia Bank put Falfurrias nearly halfway to meeting the goal for its first fund. To raise the remainder meant dialing for dollars among a list of potential investors drawn from McColl and Oken's years in banking and McColl's membership list at Augusta. There were doubters, but they also found ready interest from people like Charles S. Way Jr. of Charleston, a business titan in South Carolina with a history of making money in real estate. The development of Kiawah Island was just one of his successful ventures. Way is a double-dipped southerner who speaks with a drawl and casual familiarity. When Oken reached him, Way told him, "Don't call me Mr. Way. It's Charlie."

"He gets right to the point," Oken said, "and when I told him what I was doing he said, 'You don't need to tell me anymore. I remember back in the early eighties when my family and I were trying to raise money to do this development in Kiawah, and Hugh was there. He lent me the money when nobody else would.'" That was not the only call where Oken only had to mention McColl's name and the check was on the way.

Falfurrias filled its subscriptions by the summer of 2007 and began looking for investment opportunities. They considered candidates in a variety of markets, looking for those that fit their budget. Price was a prime consideration, since the fund agreements limited how much of the $97 million the two ultimately raised could go to one deal. Two early purchases demonstrated the range of choices. The first was a granite and marble fabricator serving home builders, and the other was a Rock Hill, South Carolina, firm that provided consulting services to utility companies. It was the third deal, though, that everyone would remember.

Little that took place in Uptown Charlotte under Hugh McColl's watch at the bank raised the city's national reputation more than the arrival of the Carolina Panthers, Charlotte's entry in the National Football League. He is pictured above in 2016 with Panthers owner Jerry Richardson in the Bank of America Stadium. (From The Charlotte Observer. © 2016 McClatchy. All rights reserved. Used under license.)

Bojangles' restaurants, a home-grown fast-food franchiser, sold spicy chicken and buttermilk biscuits. There were other regional menu items, but the Cajun-style chicken and biscuits were the focus. The first store opened in 1977 at the corner of a busy intersection at South Tryon Street and West Boulevard in a working-class neighborhood that McColl drove by countless times on his way to Douglas International Airport.

Landing Bojangles' would give Falfurrias something to talk about. It was a recognizable name with 386 outlets in eleven states, Mexico, and Honduras. Sales in 2006 were more than $500 million. That was an improvement over the prior year, but the company was having its troubles, including a crowded menu and an overextended market. The problem was that Bojangles' was a real whale whose numbers were well beyond what McColl and Oken could do on their own. When Oken brought Bojangles' to McColl's attention, it looked like a great opportunity, but only if they could find a partner to join in and help them close the deal. McColl thought he had just the guy.

McColl turned to his old friend Jerry Richardson, the owner of the Carolina Panthers. The two had been doing business together since the 1960s, when McColl arranged a $25,000 loan from NCNB that allowed Richardson and a partner to buy their first fast-food franchise, a Hardee's restaurant in Spartanburg, South Carolina. Thirty years later, McColl's command of NationsBank made it possible for Richardson to secure an NFL franchise. It was one of McColl's bright young lieutenants, Ed Brown, who devised a plan that enabled Richardson and committed fans to raise the $150 million needed to build the stadium that now carried Bank of America's name and logo over the main entrance.

The football franchise made Richardson a billionaire, but his lifetime investment was founded on fast food. Since those early days in Spartanburg he had parlayed that one Hardee's store into a food service empire called Flagstar. By the mid-1990s the company operated restaurants under the name of Denny's, Quincy's Family Steakhouse, and El Pollo Loco. In addition, it was the largest Hardee's franchisee in the country. At the time McColl called him, Richardson also owned thirty-seven Bojangles' restaurants. He signed on with Falfurrias, and with additional investors Richardson brought along, the new owners took a sixty percent stake in the company.

The Bojangles' deal turned into a genuine winner. The $50 million stake in 2007 was worth about $300 million four years later when Falfurrias cashed out. McColl's share alone was worth about $15 million. "Bojangles' was what everybody talks about," McColl said some years later. "We hit a home run. It caught everybody's attention."

The deal did more than establish credibility for Falfurrias. It brought Hugh McColl out of a deep funk. In 2008, as the nation's financial system headed toward a meltdown, he found himself powerless and unable to get out of the way of the Great Recession that robbed him of $150 million.

Chapter Four
The Earth Moved

NEARLY A DECADE passed after Hugh McColl's retirement before he again enjoyed the view from the top floor of the Bank of America Corporate Center. Even with access to the executive dining room on the fifty-eighth floor, he chose to lunch with McColl Partners analysts at blue-collar cafés. If he was looking for something a little more upscale, he often chose to eat at 300 East, a casual restaurant in a Craftsman-style house, in the Dilworth neighborhood south of Uptown.

McColl had afforded his successor, Kenneth D. Lewis, the same crisp, military respect extended him twenty-plus years earlier when Thomas I. Storrs stepped down from command of what was then NCNB. "The simplest way to put it," McColl said, "is that I walked away from the bank, and walked away mentally and physically." He was tired of the job's unrelenting claim on his time, on his life. Even with all the power that came with his job, it had never brought him true freedom.

The past, however, could not be entirely out of mind. His stock portfolio was narrow and deep, with more than two million Bank of America shares. He entered retirement invested in only three companies: his bank—it was always "his bank"; Sonoco Corporation, a South Carolina firm where he had a long-standing personal relationship; and CSX, the railroad company, where he had a seat on the board that he inherited in 1992 through family connections dating to the nineteenth century. In both the latter instances, he held only the requisite shares to qualify as a director.

> "I wanted to succeed because I had to."
>
> —Hugh McColl

McColl was agnostic about investors' faith in diversity. He ignored it out of caution over conflicts of interest or the appearance of the same. Simple as his one-stock strategy was, it had produced results. As he left for retirement, he was anticipating annual dividends of $5 million or more that he planned to use to underwrite his Chapter Two. He had no doubt his financial future was secure.

McColl comfortably eased into the role of Charlotte's corporate elder statesman, a role he came by honestly. Building on the foundation laid by his predecessors, whom he credited fulsomely and often, McColl had turned an up-and-coming regional bank into an international powerhouse. Along the way he became one of the best-known businessmen in the nation. *Forbes* and *Fortune* magazines put his picture on their covers, creating a level of notoriety that, on occasion, surprised even him. One morning in San Francisco in 1998, he was talking late pre-merger details with BankAmerica's CEO, David Coulter, in a downtown pocket park. Coulter had suggested the out-of-the-way location to avoid their being spotted at his headquarters. The two were seated side by side on a bench when a man wearing a faded military fatigue jacket approached and asked, "Aren't you Hugh McColl?" Surprised by both the visitor and his question, McColl allowed that he was. "Well, I have always wanted to meet you," the man said. He extended his hand, McColl shook it, and then the stranger turned and walked away, ignoring McColl's offer to introduce him to Coulter, San Francisco's most familiar banker.

Looking back on it all some years later, McColl attributed much of his success to timing. In 1959, when he arrived in Charlotte, it wasn't clear that it was the right place or the right time. He and Jane were newly married and so strapped for cash that they counted on Jane's father for a washing machine and a hand-me-down car. (McColl's own father's financial support had ended when he got his college degree.) He warned Jane not to get too settled in their apartment, since the job that had brought them to

Charlotte, pushed on him by his father, might not work out. He dashed about South Carolina on the bank's business in an inexpensive Volkswagen. "I was driven by need," he said. "Nobody believes I wanted to succeed because I had to."

At the time, banking was a dull business presided over by gray-headed men wounded by the Great Depression. Minimizing risk was paramount. A late 1950s survey showed the most exciting thing to happen to banking was air conditioning. The creation of Christmas Club accounts, where borrowers set aside a few dollars each week to cover the expenses of the holiday, was the height of innovation. Not long before McColl started work in Charlotte, a leading banker agreed to installment loans for automobiles as long as customers parked their new cars at the bank and left them there until the money was repaid.

Bankers of that day had come of age enjoying modest wealth and slow but steady growth. "They were all afraid of their shadow," McColl said, recollecting that time. "The people running institutions were very, very conservative and didn't like to make decisions. I came out of a background where I'd always been the person making decisions. That coupled with having been a Marine officer, where you are trained to make decisions, sent me to the top fast."

Fortunately for McColl, his father had arranged for him to join an outfit that was under the command of Addison H. Reese, a charismatic leader and the founding CEO of North Carolina National Bank. For Reese, banking was a zero-sum business when he set out to unseat Wachovia Bank and Trust Company, based in Winston-Salem, as the state's leading financial institution. As it happened, he was looking for ambitious young warriors to help him use North Carolina's liberal laws regarding bank branching to expand NCNB west to Asheville and east to Raleigh through a succession of strategic acquisitions. McColl thrived in such an environment. The strategy remained unchanged under Reese's successor, Tom Storrs, who surprised his competitors by taking NCNB to Florida and launching an era of interstate banking.

McColl acknowledges that his career succeeded for many reasons over which he had no control. In addition to his timely arrival in Charlotte, he was a white male with a good college education. In that day and time, as far as banking was concerned, no others need apply. Women worked at the teller windows but not on the loan platforms or in the executive offices, except to meet clerical needs. The only African Americans on the payroll were maintenance workers or janitors. "So we came with a lot of things going for us," McColl said. "Education, confidence, a feeling that Americans can do anything because we had won World War II. We came with the opposite of what the people who were there had. It allowed us early on to take charge of things. I was very irreverent [about the competition], because they were people to be irreverent about. They weren't very aggressive, and they were timid. They were unwilling to change."

He also joined a crowd where young men with his drive and ambition were chosen, trained, and then given their head. "What was driving us intellectually was expansion, and we had no fear of managing it because we were already managing it. We respected no one's right to have the business. We took business from people. We had a totally different view of the world and the people running the industry. They were vulnerable to us because they didn't understand being attacked. They had no defense mechanism. Yes, we had a huge advantage. It was attitudinal."

In 2001, when McColl left for retirement, it appeared that perhaps the years of consolidation were at an end. The way he saw it as he prepared to depart, the time had come for a leader who would iron out the kinks and make the mergers effected during his watch as profitable as they had been advertised. It was time for a CEO like Ken Lewis, the man he had dispatched again and again to pull the pieces together, first in Texas, then in Georgia, and later in Florida.

Lewis followed that story line for a couple of years before he rekindled the bank's expansionist fires and set out on a series of mergers of his own. The results were unsettling to McColl, but he withheld public criticism. Especially troubling were the changes Lewis made to Bank of America's board of directors in order to close the Fleet Boston Financial Corporation merger in 2003. That deal, a stock swap valued at $47 billion, installed Bank of America in New England and opened up New York City as a new market. It looked great on paper, but when a *Charlotte Observer* reporter stopped McColl at a civic fund-raising event, he gave only faint praise. "I'm a large shareholder, and I think it's a good acquisition, so I think that answers that question."

McColl did not give voice to his deep concern that in gaining New England Lewis had lessened the bank's ties to Charlotte. McColl took great pride in having turned his hometown into the nation's number-two financial center after enduring years of disdain from those who considered southerners dumb rubes with funny accents. McColl and his tribe had changed the face of American banking, and everyone was reminded of that each time they dialed the 704 area code to do business.

But the Fleet Boston deal loosened Bank of America's southern anchor. Two of the casualties in a reshuffling of the board of directors were Charlotteans John R. Belk, whom McColl had added to the board in 2001, and Frank Dowd IV. A member of the Belk and Dowd families had filled board seats since NCNB was founded in 1960. In making the changes, Lewis mollified the Boston crowd as well as critics who held that the bank's board was too heavily weighted with southerners. It was a shift in power that would later come back to haunt Lewis.

It may have been easy for Lewis to make such a concession as his ties to Charlotte were transactional, not personal. Though he, too, had been born, raised, and educated in the South, and for much of his career had lived in Charlotte, Charlotte was the place where he worked; it was not where he had invested himself. Ironically, that may have been McColl's fault since he kept sending Lewis out of North Carolina to manage new acquisitions.

McColl took consolation that the Fleet merger left the bank's headquarters right where he had built it, in the center of Uptown Charlotte. And, further, people were making money. Under Lewis, the price of the bank's stock had nearly doubled in two years, raising McColl's net worth right along with it. So in his comments to the reporter asking about the Fleet deal, McColl threw in a compliment: "I'm proud of Bank of America, and I'm proud of my successor."

After the 2003 Fleet deal, Lewis acquired MBNA of Delaware, the leading credit card outfit in the country, then headed west to acquire LaSalle Bank in 2007. LaSalle was based in Michigan but did business in other midwestern states. That acquisition gave Bank of America the right to include Chicago on the letterhead.

In the fall of 2007, as McColl's Falfurrias Capital was gathering money to purchase a controlling interest in Bojangles', Lewis was taking the first steps to acquire a home mortgage machine called Countrywide Financial. A California company, Countrywide had roared out of the 1990s and into the aughts marketing billions of dollars of easy-to-write loans that didn't fit the typical model of a responsible down payment and a repayment schedule over fifteen, twenty, or thirty years. By the fall of 2007, the Countrywide's lax standards and shoddy vetting of its customers, plus a softening in the housing market, sent it into the arms of Bank of America for an infusion of cash. In January 2008 Bank of America announced it was buying Countrywide.

This deal so outraged McColl that he did something he had avoided since leaving the chairman's office. He called a former lieutenant in the bank's corporate suite. "I sent for Greg Curl [who had put the deal together]. He came to my office, and I asked him, 'What the hell are you doing?' He said, 'Don't worry about anything. We are paying $2 billion for it, and they have a net worth of $10 billion, so we are getting $8 billion worth of negative goodwill, which will be enough to cover any of the losses.' My reaction was I was disgusted with the line of reasoning. But I did not do anything else or try to stop it."

McColl had met Countrywide's founder, Angelo Mozilo, some years before on Malcolm Forbes's yacht. Mozilo was the son of a butcher from the Bronx, but as his company grew, he cultivated a persona of the perennially tanned Californian familiar with lavish living. In the mid-1990s, an award from Harvard recognized Countrywide's efforts to extend home ownership to low- and moderate-income families. But he was both Jekyll and Hyde.

In his day, McColl had dealt with other financial pirates. Chicago billionaire Sam Zell, famous for buying companies and squeezing out profits, considered McColl a close enough friend to send him a dozen or more of the custom bronze statuettes he produced each year. One arrived at McColl's office in 1999, a warning of overvalued assets. Titled "The Emperor Has No Clothes," it featured a nude wearing a golden crown and standing on an open issue of *The Wall Street Journal*. A switch on the back activated a recording of Paul Simon's "50 Ways to Leave Your Lover" replaced with Zell's lyrics: "Are There 50 Ways to Make a Billion?" Less than a year later, the dot-com bubble burst.

Acquiring Countrywide represented a dramatic change of course for McColl's Bank of America. In 2001, he had swept the decks of Countrywide's kind of lending and had put EquiCredit, a subprime lender acquired with the merger of Barnett

Banks of Florida, up for sale. While the business of making such loans could be beneficial when done the right way, McColl had been alarmed that Bank of America was buying a mortgage mill that bore no responsibility for its deals after they were repackaged as marketable securities.

The Countrywide deal closed in mid-2008 after what insiders later said was only cursory due diligence by the buyer. Afterwards, Lewis declared that Bank of America would no longer market the risky loans, whose default rates were climbing into the double digits. He tried to convince investors that the home mortgage business could drive a wave of new customers seeking other bank services. These and other assurances seemed very thin, however. McColl had tried to keep the faith and maintained the bankers' credo of a stiff upper lip in the face of financial headwinds. Appearing in March on a panel sponsored by the Charlotte Chamber of Commerce, he professed confidence in the future of Wachovia and Bank of America. Both were well capitalized, he said. But, he told a Charlotte reporter, "we're in uncharted waters." The price of Bank of America stock continued to slide, closing forty percent below its 2008 value. Share prices were barely holding at $31.99 by late June.

In September 2008, the world plummeted into the worst financial crisis since the Great Depression. In early October 2008, McColl watched the largest and most venerable financial institutions fall.

For years, Hugh and his wife Jane set aside the first half of October to celebrate their wedding anniversary. In 2008 they were celebrating in the Pacific Northwest at a delightful resort on the coast, but Hugh couldn't keep his eyes (and mind) off the reports on CNN. "It was a terrible period in my life," he said years later. "I guess at some point I became convinced that I could survive. I really went into a deep depression for a while."

McColl doesn't like to talk about those closing weeks of 2008. Jane soldiered through that dark period without pushing too hard on questions about their future. On occasion, a boorish dinner companion might allude that somehow the bank's problems were all McColl's fault. Those who knew them well said nothing. A decade later when the subject was raised, he still chose to speak in generalities.

It was embarrassing that many of the bank's troubles were connected to a company whose toxic mortgages destroyed neighborhoods. The bank had honored McColl by donating millions to Habitat for Humanity, an organization founded on simple notions of sweat equity and careful vetting of prospective homeowners to build strong neighborhoods. In the 1990s, McColl's bank had invested billions in building up neighborhoods with loans at fair and reasonable terms that built home ownership. Lewis had not only continued this investment but enlarged it even more. Community-building loans had performed well over the years; far more second mortgages to the wealthy were now in default.

In the aftermath Wachovia succumbed, and Charlotte lost a corporate headquarters as Wells Fargo took over one of the oldest names in North Carolina banking. Wachovia's distinctive new building, under construction on South Tryon Street in Charlotte, was later sold and eventually became the headquarters of Duke Energy. Lewis headed into 2009 fending off complaints over Bank of America's distress purchase of the securities firm Merrill Lynch, a transaction concluded just as the markets were failing. The liabilities from Countrywide and loan losses from credit card debt continued to climb as the value of Bank of America stock steadily fell. It finally hit a low of $3 and change. On the day President Barack Obama was inaugurated in January 2009, it had inched up to just a little more than $5 per share.

In the end, as lending standards were reduced to virtually nothing, Countrywide and businesses like it were ticking time bombs that eventually blew up, and took down the economy. Subsequent investigations highlighted egregious examples of fraud by Countrywide. The investigation of the 2008 financial crisis showed that Mozilo knew his company was issuing billions of dollars in loans that were doomed to fail even as he arranged the sale to Bank of America.

Like other high-wealth investors with intertwined and leveraged financial arrangements, McColl had no choice but to ride his Bank of America stock all the way to the bottom. Quickly restructuring a large portfolio is a challenge in good times; it is virtually impossible in bad.

The Great Recession punctured the spirit of a man who lived a life fueled by optimism. In the fall of 2008, he really wasn't sure what lay ahead. "I thought I was going to be fixed for life," he said, "and I wasn't. Falfurrias was only about a year old, and I didn't know I was going to make any money there. I had a couple of bad years."

Years later, McColl calculated his total losses at between $120 and $150 million. Even ten years on, McColl's Bank of America stock was worth about half what it had been before the calamity. In the intervening years, dividends that he had counted on to produce as much as $5 million a year disappeared, dropping from a high of sixty-four cents a share to a penny, where they remained for nearly five years before beginning to rebound. At the end of 2019, the annual dividend rate was at seventy-two cents per share.

McColl had begun cutting back on his operations before the financial crisis. Before the collapse he exited the art business, where he had invested several million dollars without making a dime. McColl flatly admits that his fondness for the work of American artists working between 1840 and 1940 was not in the mainstream for a southern market whose customers favor images of the beach or the mountains. Even his maritime art tilted to Yankee sailing ships and the rocky coastlines of Massachusetts. "I know nothing about retailing," he confessed one day, "and I showed it. I lost millions of dollars."

Alongside the financial loss of the Great Recession, there was another deep hurt that could not be measured in dollars. The strong, robust company that McColl and his team created had been brought to the very brink of destruction. In the end, Bank of America survived, unlike seven of its Tryon Street banking neighbors, large and small. While it was still standing when Lewis departed as CEO at the end of 2009 in the midst of the uncertain challenges to the nation's banks, it appeared to outsiders that Bank of America was becoming a "Charlotte" bank largely in name only. Lewis's replacement, Brian T. Moynihan, was a Boston lawyer whose career had been spent not only north of the Mason-Dixon line but in the lee of Cape Cod. And the bank's board of directors that once was said to have too much of a southern tilt? Six of the seven Fleet directors elected in 2003 still occupied their seats on the board. Only five of the twelve from the Charlotte crowd remained. Charlotte still housed the corporation's headquarters. In reality the bank's hub was wherever Moynihan's big

Gulfstream happened to be parked. More often than not, that was Boston, where he maintained his residence, or New York City.

McColl took satisfaction that Bank of America was strong enough to sustain an estimated hit of $200 billion. The Great Recession left its resources drained. Imposition of penalties and fees rose to the tens of billions, and regulators called a lot of the shots for a period of time. At least its headquarters remained at the tower on the Square, a building taller than anything else around. Yes, there was something to be said for survival.

Charlotte was rocked back on her heels. In the latter part of 2009, a *Washington Post* reporter who knew the city from his days at the *Charlotte Observer,* headlined his story: "This is the bust in the boomtown that banks built."

Lines at the Urban Ministry soup kitchen were longer; there were fewer arrivals and departures of private planes from the airport. Construction came to a halt on downtown buildings, including one condominium project that was already forty stories into the sky. Entire subdivisions were up for sale. In a city that was known as "Banktown" during the glory days that had lasted twenty years or so, the second largest bank behind Bank of America with a headquarters in Charlotte was now one with six branches and forty-nine employees. *Charlotte Observer* columnist Mary Newsome said those days were like Superman discovering kryptonite. There were layoffs at the banks and among the supporting clientele. Law firms fat with bank business began eliminating associates with ruthless efficiency. More than 50,000 jobs disappeared. Publicly supported agencies for the arts and civic welfare saw their contributions cut in half. Unemployment was high everywhere and pushed twelve percent in Charlotte.

> "Those days were like Superman discovering kryptonite."
> —Mary Newsome

City officials went to New York City in September 2008 to wrap up the sale of a package of municipal bonds. While waiting for an audience at Bank of America City Manager Curt Walton learned that Wachovia Corporation was about to be sold. His Bank of America hosts greeted the news with ashen faces. Walton expected a different reaction after years of rivalry. The stark reality of the moment did not allow for gloating over a competitor's misfortune. "It was like a mass funeral," he said.

Those who had been through the wars with McColl felt betrayed as their own stock holdings were diminished to pennies on the dollar. John Cleghorn had written speeches for McColl in the 1990s and had stayed on to manage other projects until 2008 when he left for the ministry. As the financial crisis drained his former coworkers' savings in 2009, Cleghorn opened the sanctuary at Caldwell Presbyterian for a session of what amounted to grief counseling. McColl attended and delivered a pep talk, reminding his former coworkers that they had soldiered through tough times before. "We worked on things together," he said, the memory of the moment drifting back in place. "It was a remarkable company in that way. We liked each other, and we were.... It was something." For him, the bond remained as strong as ever.

The new hard times actually worked in the city's favor. Interest rates fell to their lowest in years. The low cost of money, coupled with the hunger for construction projects, allowed the city to build and pay for projects much more cheaply than had been anticipated. In addition, when defaulted loans were taken over by lenders, the rate of tax collections improved. Banks left holding the property proved to be more reliable in their payments than the original owners. Wells Fargo would actually increase its local payroll in the years ahead.

McColl, on the sidelines solving his own problems, remained part of the conversation, both locally and nationally. He joked at one public appearance that the Obama administration dismissed his advice about fixing the economy. David Vorhoff clearly remembers when he heard McColl's cell phone ring in the midst of a client meeting. McColl tried to ignore the insistent buzzing but finally answered. It was Jane who had another caller on the line trying to reach him. *Sotto voce*, he told his wife he was busy and the caller would have to wait. Vorhoff was dumbstruck when he learned later that the other caller was someone from the White House. "How many people would tell the president, 'I'm busy?'"

McColl felt the president's people weren't impressed with his ideas. To boost the economy, he proposed an initiative of tax advantages similar to what President John F. Kennedy had used in the sixties, as well as increased depreciation to boost business.

"We were never able to get it done," he said, "because the administration was so anti-rich people that they couldn't figure out how to stimulate the economy using taxes, because in order to do that you would have to help rich people. I gave up on them. I had tried everything I knew to try."

In the summer of June 2009 Wells Fargo's CEO, John Stumpf, visited Charlotte to survey the bank's East Coast operations, including the call center on the city's north side where about 10,000 people were employed. Over dinner McColl shared with Stumpf the history of Charlotte.

About six months later, Bank of America CEO Brian Moynihan went downstairs to the fifty-first floor to meet with McColl. After that, McColl began to appear more often on the bank's behalf at various community functions, slowly transitioning into the role of Bank of America's ambassador, something of an unelected chairman emeritus.

Bashing banks remained in vogue for a long time. Someone had to be to blame for creating such a catastrophe. What was to be done to prevent this from happening again in the future? Even President Obama joined the chorus of condemnation; a commission was organized to investigate and congressional committees began work on new laws. The commission called witnesses, including Lewis and Mozilo, who returned for repeated sessions. Congress finally drafted the Dodd-Frank Wall Street Reform and Consumer Protection Act in 2010, addressing the danger of banks that had grown "too big to fail." The new regulations were the most sweeping since the Great Depression and covered everything from the solvency of financial institutions to the creation of the Consumer Finance Protection Bureau.

From McColl's view, the road to the greatest financial upheaval in seventy years was relatively straight. He attributed the problems to the greed of investment bankers who pushed the mortgage industry to produce more and more bad loans that fed into a market chasing higher and higher returns. "They came up with an idea of dicing [packages of loans] so we're only going to have 10 percent losses, so we'll have 90 percent of this paper is A paper, and 10 percent of it's F paper. The problem was they didn't know that there was no way to know which was which. And they got that all wrong. Everybody that touched it was doing it for greed. Nobody could have defended what was being done. It's just not right."

He has no patience for those who blame the lending requirements of the Community Reinvestment Act for expanding lending to low- and moderate-income borrowers and inflating the housing bubble. His bank embraced the program and turned it into a money-making machine. "We built houses and made money doing it. We were able to do charitable work, in effect, and make money at it. We didn't see it as something we had to do; it was something we wanted to do." Later research showed the Community Reinvestment Act borrowers had a far better repayment record than those gaming the system and borrowing beyond their means. "The risk quadrant," McColl said, "was people living high on the hog."

He freely takes ownership of having pushed changes in federal laws to allow the formation of large banks that eventually grew to the point that their failure was considered too much of a shock to the system and thus had to be saved by federal financial support. McColl stubbornly defended his belief that big banks, like Bank of America, were not evil simply because of their bigness. Indeed, big banks should be able to ride through the economic storms. Anyone looking for evidence of banks suffering from narrow financial interests need only consider the history of NCNB. It was able to acquire First Republic in Texas because of a collapse in oil prices when the bank had nothing to offset the losses. "When gas and oil went to $10," McColl said, "they went bankrupt. The whole state went bankrupt. They lost 50, 60, 100 billion dollars worth of net worth overnight."

All in all, Dodd-Frank was not the disaster that some bankers portrayed it to be. McColl likes the discipline imposed on investment bankers but is uneasy with the legislative response that gave renewed life and power to the risk managers, the part of the bank most inclined to say no to those calling on customers. "Now, there should be a balance in that," he says. "You should never give all the power to the salesman either. There's a balance, you've got to have a check and balance. I think what we've done is go back to the sixties, or the fifties, truthfully. That's where I see banking today, that we're right back where we started.

"The problem always is they close the barn door after the horse is out, but then a new problem erupts. And I think there's general agreement about what the next problem is going to be. By making it difficult for the banks to be lenders, by making the banks jump through so many hoops, the banks are less responsive to the public than they were, particularly to the poor people. In other words, if you are looking at the people you're really trying to get money to, they haven't got a chance in hell of getting a loan from a bank.

"So it has allowed non-bank lenders to develop, who are not regulated, and who don't know what they're doing, and who will cause the next big collapse. In other words, the next big collapse will be caused by the collapse of non-bank lenders. It'll happen. Sure as hell going to happen."

Falfurrias cashed out of Bojangles' in 2011 with what McColl calls a "big, big win." Most would agree that an investment of $50 million that turned into $300 million in three years would so qualify. McColl's share of $15 million didn't come close to filling the hole created by the devaluation of his Bank of America stock, but it helped. More important, it was a confidence builder. The clouds were beginning to lift. Falfurrias immediately set about raising money for a second fund, which would be followed by a third and a fourth by 2020, with each one larger than the last.

In 2013 McColl Partners was sold to Deloitte for an undisclosed sum. "We really became quite successful. That business lasted thirteen years. We sold it in 2013 because it had the disease that every investment bank gets, which is that the big producers think they should be paid more money, a lot more money, no matter how much you pay them, and they're jealous of each other. It's a sad treatise on the business.

"The six men that came in with me probably averaged making a million dollars a year during their entire time there with me. When it first started, they were only being paid $48,000, but within a few years, they were making a half a million dollars a year and then started making a million, a million-five. So we made good money. We took a business, built it from nothing, and made $50 million a year."

"So I'm over it," he allowed one sunny morning in the late fall of 2019. "When you are older you think you need more money than you need. The only money I need today, or I should say the money I miss having, is the additional money that I could give away. I think I've told you I've never given away a dollar I missed or paid a dollar in taxes that I missed."

Chapter Five
Raising Money

ONCE AGAIN the Charlotte Symphony Orchestra was in financial trouble. But this time was different. The near-total collapse of the nation's financial system in 2008 had inflicted substantial damage on donors' pocketbooks. The income for nonprofits like the CSO had been reduced to a trickle. Corporate support was problematic; patrons who once pledged based on profits and dividends generated by their stock portfolios were traumatized by astonishing losses. The symphony's future was in doubt, and this time talk of its demise wasn't hyperbole.

Hugh and Jane McColl had heard this death rattle before. It was hard to remember when the symphony wasn't on their list of Charlotte institutions to support, and they had responded to earlier days of crisis and need. Hugh's artistic tastes actually ran more to dance, particularly the athleticism of ballet and modern dance, but if Jane liked the symphony, he was a fan, too. She was a former member of the CSO's board of directors, and it didn't take long for word to reach her that the million dollars the organization was expecting from the Arts and Sciences Council wasn't coming. The ASC, Charlotte's principal funder for arts groups large and small, was cutting back. Its two principal benefactors and their employees, the Bank of America and the bank formerly known as Wachovia (before it was consumed by Wells Fargo), weren't going to be forwarding the piles of cash they had in the past. Bankers and the thousands of people they employed in Charlotte had more pressing things on their minds. These two "rich uncles"—that's what Hugh later called them—had higher priorities than keeping the arts alive in Charlotte.

Jonathan Martin knew when he became the CSO's executive director in spring 2008 that he was in for a rebuilding job. The symphony had struggled financially for several years, but now the puddle of red ink had members of his board believing the CSO could never set itself aright. Martin wasn't the only new face around the place. Christopher Warren-Green was on his way to the city as the orchestra's new music director. Though Martin hadn't planned on welcoming him with a request that he take an immediate pay cut, when he did Warren-Green said he understood and cinched his belt.

The CSO wasn't just another arts organization. It was one of Charlotte's first. Some called it the "campfire around which everyone else gathers." Indeed, it had been active since early 1932, when native Spaniard, Guilliermo S. de Roxlo, pulled together thirty or so amateur musicians and began rehearsing pieces by Mozart, Wagner, and Debussy in the auditorium of Central High School, the scene of the first concert on March 21. A tall, lean man, de Roxlo composed a few modest works of his own but was best known locally as the private teacher of violin and piano for those with latent musical talent just waiting for the right moment. Well-regarded in town, he carried off an air befitting a maestro. His narrow face was anchored by a strong and prominent chin, his high forehead framed by the swirls of an impressive pompadour. It was reported that four thousand people turned out July 8 for the free concert de Roxlo's CSO played at the amphitheater in Independence Park.

The symphony held itself together through the Great Depression, and by the late thirties de Roxlo had recruited as the CSO's president and leading patron Mrs. Cameron Morrison (née Sara Watts), one of the city's richest women. She was the widow of Durham tobacco millionaire George W. Watts when she married Governor Morrison, himself a widower, in 1924. The newlyweds moved into an expansive country home they built in Charlotte called Morrocroft. With Mrs. Morrison's help, de Roxlo expanded the symphony's headcount to nearly fifty players on the eve of

World War II. It was equally strong a decade later when it was led by music director Lamar Stringfield, the man who had brought the North Carolina Symphony Orchestra to life in 1932.

To some, the symphony's 2009 ASC pay cut looked like the beginning of the final chapter of the orchestra's history. Reducing its annual grant was an implied rebuke of the symphony's management. The criticism was not aimed at Martin, the symphony's new executive director, so much as the CSO's five-plus money-losing seasons. Additionally, ASC was facing a 37 percent cut in its own income, and as the symphony had received the lion's share of ASC funds in the past, it would suffer equally on the downside. The symphony was told it would have to find the money it needed to continue in business and produce a business plan before receiving any further ASC support.

If the CSO and its sponsors were unable to drag the symphony out of its financial quagmire, it might be time for the city's classical music lovers to settle for less. The notion of a smaller orchestra with amateur players was entertained, recalling Guillermo and his volunteer musicians and the glowing reviews they'd received in the thirties. If it had worked then, why not now?

Hugh McColl didn't dwell on all this backstory. The symphony had survived Hard Times, World War II, and years of performing in Ovens Auditorium, a place where "sound went to die," before he had led the efforts to construct an acoustically balanced replacement. Determined to see the CSO through the nation's second-worst financial calamity in modern times, he organized something designed to stifle talk of the CSO's demise. In September 2009, along with C. D. "Dick" Spangler Jr., Hugh and Jane pledged a million-dollar donation to underwrite the symphony's operation. Their support removed any doubt hanging over the viability of the upcoming season.

It was well-known around the city, especially among those heavily invested in the hometown banks, that both Spangler and McColl had taken huge hits in the financial crisis. Spangler's losses on his Bank of America holdings alone amounted to more than half a billion dollars. For two of the city's most prominent men of business to step forward at this time was a validation that the symphony literally could take to the bank. "It was a huge statement," Martin said some years later. "And it wasn't just about the money."

"The money put a stop to talk within the ASC that perhaps it was time for the symphony to throw in the towel," Martin remembers. "There was a fair amount of skepticism among the arts community, starting with the ASC, about the efficacy and viability of the orchestra going forward. They would hear from smaller organizations that ASC was giving 'too much money' to CSO. The CSO was on life support, and they needed to restructure and turn into an orchestra half its size.

"Hugh never bought into it. He knew that once you started that downward spiral, you couldn't just call it a day and balance the budget. It doesn't work that way. You basically have to stop and Chapter 7 yourself out of existence and let the venom dissipate, which takes years. Then you start over. That was not a scenario that either he or I thought was in the best interest of the city of Charlotte."

To accept anything less than a fully functional, professional body of musicians was contrary to everything that the McColls believed about the symphony's place in Charlotte. Any city with a bright and shiny future—and Hugh had spent his career building Charlotte into such a place—needed a symphony to attract the kind of people who would be interested in jobs at its banks or the corporations that Charlotte was bringing to town. The symphony was a symbol of the strength of the community's support for the arts. Furthermore, losing the symphony would diminish the pleasure of enjoying a broad array of the arts. The opera and the ballet would be left without reliable and worthy accompaniment. The loss would clearly reduce the community of musicians who called Charlotte home and limit the penetration of music of all kinds, not just the classical repertoire, into the life of the region, from the schools to the churches. If Charlotte were to have a place among the leading cities of the nation, then a symphony was a must. "The Charlotte Symphony is the sound of the city," Jane said when the million-dollar gift was announced.

For Hugh it was equally as basic, but it was never really just about the music. In fact, he believes he's a bit tone deaf. He enjoys some pieces, but midway through others he can hear an inner voice asking, "How much longer is this going to last?" For years, many had the same question when the CSO's performances were at Ovens Auditorium, a multipurpose hall built in the 1950s that did nothing to enhance the voice of the symphony. As the *Charlotte Observer*'s Richard Maschal put it in 1988, "Performing Beethoven's Fifth or Verdi's 'La Traviata' in Ovens Auditorium with its poor acoustics is like putting chardonnay in a Coke bottle."

Hugh had seen to it that part of the $300 million complex surrounding the base of NCNB's corporate headquarters was designed for music making. The 2,100-seat Belk Theater inside the Blumenthal Center for the Performing Arts which opened May 1992 incorporated the very best acoustics and sight lines. The McColls enjoyed the benefits of international expert Richard Pilbrow's precise design from the "Queen's Seats," a pair of seats in the middle of first row in the Grand Tier said to be the best in the house. In retirement McColl relinquished the seats to the bank and moved four spaces to the side.

McColl knew that the donation he made with Spangler in 2009 was "a thumb in the dike." That nagged at him, and later on, he met with Michael Marsicano, the head of the Foundation For The Carolinas, in a downtown bistro. The two had worked together on behalf of the arts for two decades or more. In 1995, when Marsicano was running the ASC, McColl had chaired an extraordinary campaign that raised a $25 million endowment for the arts. The National Endowment for the Arts rewarded this head-turning effort with an $800,000 grant. That campaign arose, in part, out of another economic recession, this one in the early 1990s, that left the symphony and other organizations gasping for life. The 1995 campaign was meant to secure the financial future of the arts in Charlotte. Hugh and Jane put in $1 million. NationsBank did $3 million more.

Over a glass of wine, McColl asked Marsicano how many times the two had arranged a financial lifeline. Five times? Six times? Well, no matter. "I'm going to do it one more time," McColl told Marsicano. "I'm going to raise enough to sustain the symphony for ten years." McColl figured that in ten years he'd be dead and gone and the symphony would be someone else's problem. If the symphony needed about $2 million annually to make its budget, then his goal was $20 million. That was a bold number, but doable enough. Furthermore, he was going to tackle this alone. He didn't want any fanfare, no announcements, he told Marsicano, and no committee. It would just be him and his tin cup, working on his own schedule and in his own way.

Giving money away is something McColl thoroughly enjoys. Raising money from others is another thing entirely, although his philanthropic record gives him an edge. "I've raised quite a bit of money, but I guess I have primed the pump. We have cast bread on the water. I don't mind asking some people for money because I have given away a lot myself."

Ever the banker, McColl sees money as a tool. It is no good unless it is put to use. Money makes the world work, and even unexpected windfalls are ushered into service. Two young entrepreneurs called on him one day and told him they had a check for a million dollars with his name on it. They were closing a multi-billion-dollar deal on a company they created. The check was a thank you for the lessons they had learned at his elbow. "The hell you say," McColl responded. "You're not

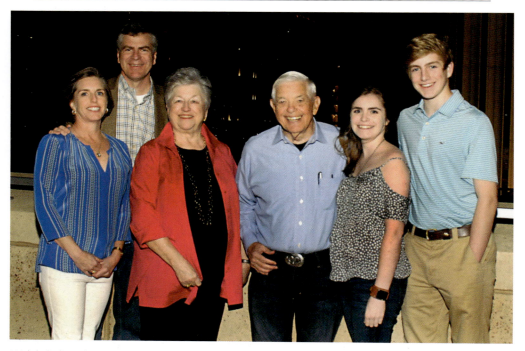

With help from the community and friends, the McColl family has underwritten research in limb-girdle muscular dystrophy 2i, a rare disease that afflicts Hugh and Jane's granddaughter, Jane B. Lockwood. The McColl-Lockwood Laboratory in Charlotte, established through the Carolinas Muscular Dystrophy Research, part of Atrium Health, was created by the McColl and Lockwood families to find a cure for the disease. Pictured here from left to right are the McColl's daughter Jane M. Lockwood, her husband Luther Lockwood, Jane and Hugh, granddaughter Jane B., and grandson Thomas Lockwood. (Photo courtesy of the McColl family)

giving me a million dollars," he told them. If they wanted to give away money, then they could send it to support research into limb-girdle muscular dystrophy 2i, a rare disease that afflicts his granddaughter Jane B. Lockwood. They did. The money helped underwrite work that includes bringing all the top research doctors in the world to Charlotte to share ideas and provoke intellectual stimulation around the disease. "We've moved the ball," McColl says.

McColl can be casual about money. He says he's not sure how much he has at his personal disposal. His son Hugh III looks after all that. It's not that he doesn't care. Rather, he remains inspired to do deals and rake in profits because good years mean he has more money to give away. And he prefers his hip-pocket style of philanthropy even though there is a family foundation his daughter, Jane M. Lockwood, looks after. As for himself, that's all too cumbersome and inhibits the spontaneity of responding to needs as they arise such as the emergency aid he gave Debra Orock Enoru.

A native of Cameroon, Enoru was a junior at Queens University and interning at McColl Partners back in 2003 when she learned her tuition bills were long overdue. The registrar wanted money immediately. In tears, she confided to a coworker she'd probably have to leave her job and drop out. David Sheffer, one of the firm's analysts, advised her to talk to McColl. He was chair of the Queens trustees. Perhaps he could help.

Enoru had exchanged little more than a welcoming nod with McColl. Even approaching his office and asking Pat Hinson for an appointment took all the courage she could muster. She prevailed on Sheffer to come along for moral support. Once inside McColl's office, she told her story. McColl listened and then asked about the American family that had helped her come to the United States, helped her enroll at Queens, and now was unable to pay her bills. He wanted to know about her country in West Africa, the progress of her studies at Queens, and the plans she had for a career. The wide-ranging conversation ended with him opening his checkbook and handing her a check to pay the $16,000 due the university.

Enoru was stunned. Twenty years later, that moment was still breathtaking to recall. "I told him, 'Sir, I don't know how I can ever replay you. I don't know what to do.' I said, 'I am going to work for this money, and I will pay you back.' He said,

'Debra, calm down.' I was hysterical. I had never known that level of generosity. He said, 'I don't want you to ever pay me back. What I want you to do, if you are ever in a position, is to help someone else. Debra, you have to do that.' Those words have never left me. Those words live and are part of my life experiences and things I do in my life. Those words are still in my head."

Enoru graduated with her class, qualified for advanced studies in England, and then settled in Washington, D.C., where she became an analyst for the board of governors of the Federal Reserve System. She later wrote McColl to fill him in on how her life had unfolded. Her husband was a cardiologist; they had two children. "I tell my kids the story of what you did for me to instill the character of service to others even at such a young age," she wrote. "You will always be an integral and unforgettable part of my life."

McColl prefers the privacy of such benevolence. He doesn't make noise with his philanthropy. There are few institutions in Charlotte that haven't been touched by his gifts, but public recognition is subdued. One exception is the McColl Center for Art + Innovation, the artist-in-residence facility created within the walls of a burned-out church on North Tryon Street that McColl and Bank of America saved from oblivion. For nearly two decades, the center has served artists from around the country. The name recognizes that Hugh made it possible, but it's there also as a tribute to his mother, the artist.

McColl freely admits his style of fund-raising runs contrary to that of most professionals. His list of potential donors grows from personal history. He doesn't plan visits so much as he looks for opportunities to present his case. Then he seizes the occasion and "picks his victim's pocket." During the arts endowment campaign, he found himself on an elevator with two of Charlotte's richest men, Dick Spangler and Alan Dickson, one of his bank's directors and co-founder of the Ruddick Corporation, where McColl himself was a director. By the time the elevator car reached the ground floor McColl had million-dollar pledges from each of them. "I raised two million dollars in forty seconds," he says. "I don't like to make appointments. I just catch people. It works better when it's casual and in conversation." He waits for the right time and confesses he's ready when "people make the mistake of asking what you are working on."

That's largely the story of how he got $10 million from Bank of America to put toward securing the symphony's future. It was early in 2010, and the bank's new CEO, Brian T. Moynihan, was a stranger to Charlotte. So when the new chairman made his first trip south, he asked McColl if he could stop by for an introductory visit. Paying a courtesy call on the bank's most prominent alumnus was bound to help settle the nerves of those who expected Moynihan, a Bostonian, to begin relocating entire departments and bank functions to precincts up North. The two men talked awhile, and as Moynihan rose to take his leave, he asked McColl if there was anything he could do for him.

McColl was ready. "Yes, you can give me $10 million for saving the symphony," he told Moynihan. He briefly explained the situation and his plan for the future. Moynihan paused, and then McColl heard him say, "'Well, I'll have to check. I'll have to check with my people.' And I said, 'Who are you going to ask?' I mean, he's the CEO." Taking this lesson in leadership, Moynihan confirmed the bank's commitment before he departed.

At the time of Moynihan's visit, McColl already had a pledge for $2.5 million from Leon Levine, a merchant who had opened his first Family Dollar store on Charlotte's east side in 1959. By 2010 he had 7,000 or so of them spread all across the nation. He and McColl had a history of reciprocity in support of community good deeds. Levine's response to McColl's pitch for the symphony was to suggest that they round up nine others who, like him, would put up $2.5 million each. That didn't fit McColl's strategy, but he was feeling pretty good about his efforts so far. He had made two calls and picked up commitments for $12.5 million. More than halfway toward his goal and feeling the momentum, he called the office of Jim Rogers, the CEO at Duke Energy, found he was available, and headed out the door.

McColl was very familiar with the trek down South Tryon Street to Duke's headquarters. It was almost like old times, when Rogers's predecessor, the late Bill Lee, was one of McColl's mates in civic endeavors. The two were half of a clique of business titans that people once called "The Group." The other regulars were Rolfe Neill, publisher of the *Charlotte Observer,* and First Union CEO Ed Crutchfield.

Former Mayor John Belk was asked to join in on special occasions, mainly to hold down any negativity that might arise from his corner. Lee and McColl had worked hand in hand to build the symphony's concert hall inside the Blumenthal Center for the Performing Arts, which stood on the site where the Belk family's retail empire began. The $20 million Lee raised in private donations for the center was combined with support from the city and about $15 million from the state government. McColl wheedled the latter out of Raleigh with the help of Democrats in the legislature who were eager for his political backing. It didn't hurt that Joe Martin, a key player on McColl's team at the bank, was the brother of the Republican governor, Jim Martin.

Jim Rogers was a newcomer to the city, having arrived in 2006 as the product of Duke's merger with Cinergy Corporation, a power and gas company serving the Midwest. He moved from Cincinnati, Ohio, a city with a storied and deep appreciation of the arts and a symphony dating back to 1894. McColl, hoping for an ally, met with Rogers. But after an hour spent only answering questions, he had a sinking feeling. This is a water haul; I'm wasting both our time, he thought.

"Then somewhere he sensed my itchiness," McColl said, recalling the visit a decade later. "What do you need?" Rogers asked. "Ten million dollars," McColl answered, feeling bold after seeing Moynihan. "I'll tell you what I am going to do," Rogers said. "I will give you two and a half million personally, and the [Duke Energy] foundation will give you $10 million." McColl felt pretty good as he headed back up Tryon Street. Once in his office he called Marsicano to tell him he had the symphony's $20 million and then some, all within a matter of weeks.

For McColl, the results represented more than a reprieve for the symphony. There was an unexpected personal reward—his success affirmed his place in Charlotte. Before he retired, he'd predicted that in five years he'd be long forgotten. Even within the company he had built, they'd soon stop taking his calls. That had never played out. McColl "sightings" in the bank still sent emails flying from employees at every level. So here he was, nearly ten years into retirement, on his first outing in aid of a major civic enterprise, and he was discovering that as a civilian he still had the capacity to get people to follow his lead. All those years before, he could count on his coworkers to follow when "his bank" boosted community projects, which it usually kicked off with the largest gift. This private campaign for the symphony demonstrated that he could still make a difference.

The campaign could have ended there, but Marsicano urged McColl to consider staying the course to raise an endowment that would serve other arts organizations. The financial crisis had exposed the arts community's vulnerability of relying on corporate giving and employee payroll checkoffs. While both of these income streams had produced some of the highest levels of charitable giving in the nation, for the arts and for the United Way, funding for both the cultural and the social welfare of the community now faced new challenges. Nonprofits knew that when the economy recovered they could not expect a return to that old model.

"The symphony would not be here without Hugh McColl. It's just that simple."

—BOB STICKLER

With Marsicano's support, McColl pushed on, again at his own pace, taking only clerical support from the foundation, which became the depository for the harvest. Over the coming year or more he collected more pledges, and the goal began inching higher. Some responded without McColl's even making a specific request. Over lunch one day with Jerry Richardson, the owner of the Carolina Panthers, McColl shared the things that were keeping him busy. The next day one of Richardson's assistants called to say her boss's $2.5 million pledge was on the way.

McColl's efforts became public three years in. The *Charlotte Observer* reported in July 2014 the campaign (now called Thrive) had raised $34 million; by the end of the year the fund totaled $37 million. The Foundation For The Carolinas managed the assets, while the distributions were determined by a governing board composed of representatives from Thrive's largest donors. The first round of grants amounted to $3.1 million and, in addition to the symphony, provided supplemental funding for the Charlotte Ballet, Opera Carolina, and the Children's Theater of Charlotte.

In 2012, Jonathan Martin left unexpectedly to become the general manager at the Dallas Symphony. McColl urged Bob Stickler, who had just stepped down from

Bank of America, to forego whatever retirement plans he may have and serve as the symphony's interim executive director. Stickler had been on the symphony board since 2008 representing the symphony's choral partner, the Oratorio Singers of Charlotte. That fall, on a rainy Saturday, he reviewed the CSO balance sheets with McColl. Their banking experience made it clear that even the $2 million from Thrive would not be sufficient to cover the expected loss in his first year on the job.

Stickler used the financial stimulus from Thrive to rebuild the organization so that it could end fiscal 2014 in the black. But to get there, everyone took a hit. The musicians signed a three-year contract at reduced compensation. Stickler cut his own pay, as did the remaining staff. He also convinced the symphony's landlord, the Blumenthal Performing Arts Center, to hold rent steady for three years, and then he launched a push to raise money from the symphony board and the community. "The symphony would not be here without Hugh McColl. It's just that simple," said Stickler.

Music Director Christopher Warren-Green was all in during what he described as a "very scary two years." He and his musicians adjusted to the new reality and accepted all manner of invitations to perform at special events that showcased the symphony, reminding Charlotteans of the organization's value.

Warren-Green and his wife, violinist Rosemary Furniss, in gratitude for the McColl's support, invited Jane and Hugh to home-cooked meals topped off with Rosemary's specialty, bread and butter pudding, "an artery-hardening confection" whose recipe Furniss brought with her from England. Over dinner one night, Jamie, the couple's shy eight-year-old son, surprised his parents and their guests and offered to play something on his clarinet. Jamie's impromptu solo performance might have had something to do with McColl's offer to build Jamie a tree house. On their way home afterwards, Jane reminded her husband of his promise. A few years before he had built a treehouse in his own backyard big enough to host three generations of McColls at a sixtieth birthday breakfast. McColl was prepared to deliver.

Jamie Warren-Green's tree house was built "to code" by members of McColl's old Habitat crew, including Brenda Suits and eight or nine other volunteers. Due to limited arboreal options, the resulting design was a tree house in name only. It stood atop four pillars set in concrete in a cove of trees, none of which would support an actual tree house. The resulting structure was outfitted with fully functional glass windows, retractable stairs with hand railings, and a chimney for a stove. The labor stretched over several midsummer weekends featuring high humidity and temperatures pushing a hundred degrees. One day, Jane, alarmed when her husband hadn't answered his phone, called Suits. "Brenda, please tell me, dear God y'all are not out here building in this. They're telling on the news the elderly should not be out in the heat, and he's elderly." Suits passed her phone to Hugh, who chatted briefly with his wife. When the call ended he turned to Suits and asked, "Did she call me elderly?"

A few years prior to organizing his private fundraising effort on behalf of the Charlotte Symphony Orchestra, Hugh and Jane McColl led a campaign to raise nearly $10 million to build and endow a permanent home for the Charlotte Ballet. The groundbreaking in 2009 took place in Uptown Charlotte adjacent to the renovated church that houses the McColl Center for Art + Innovation. Holding ceremonial shovels in 2009 and standing between the McColls are Patricia McBride, the ballet's former artistic director, and former associate artistic director Jean-Pierre Bonnefoux. (Photo by Jeff Cravotta, courtesy of the Charlotte Ballet)

Ten years later, the Warren-Greens were no longer in the neighborhood, but the tree house was still standing. "It will take a bulldozer to bring it down," said McColl. "A tornado won't move this tree house."

Warren-Green rewarded those early symphony donors by arranging invitations to Buckingham Palace. Using connections made when he had directed London's Philharmonia Orchestra at the Prince of Wales' wedding to Camilla Parker Bowles, Warren-Green saw that the Charlotteans were included in a gala display of artistic talent, from acting and ballet to classical music. The McColls and the Levines traveled with the Spanglers to London on the Spanglers' new jet. After the performances they enjoyed dinner in the palace's Picture Gallery and mingled with the new Duchess of Cornwall and the prince. Spangler was disappointed that his highness failed to remember a visit he had made to Biltmore Estate some years earlier. Neither did he recall his photo on the cover of a posh magazine on English homes that Jane had read on the way over. In parting, she told the prince, "I'll send it to you." She did and got a thank you note in reply. Her husband also got a $25,000 bill for the evening. Apparently the event was a fund-raiser, something the Americans were unaware of when they flew across the pond.

The success of the Thrive Campaign capped one of the most productive periods of McColl's civic life. Over the years, he had used his bank and its resources to reshape the center of Charlotte, constructing buildings and sponsoring the arts. He had raised money for the arts overall and for specific areas of interest. The Charlotte ballet gained a building of its own thanks to his and Jane's generosity and fund-raising efforts. But nothing compared to what he accomplished with Thrive. Marsicano, who makes his living guiding and managing philanthropy, said, "The reason Thrive is so significant, is because of the amount of money and because McColl did it himself." When *Charlotte* magazine picked its superlatives for 2014, it singled him out for his contribution to the arts.

A profile of McColl written by the magazine's editor, Michael Graff, appeared in the November 14, 2014, issue. Unknown to most everyone at the time the story was published, McColl was in a Charlotte hospital, with Jane and the rest of the family marveling that he was still alive.

Some months earlier, McColl had taken a tumble after a trio of small dogs surprised him on Litchfield Beach in South Carolina. Some weeks after the fall, he began experiencing minor problems in walking, such as dragging a foot. Doctors examined his spine and lower torso, thinking the problem was there. They found nothing, and the troubling symptoms grew steadily worse. On a trip to Italy in early October, Jane grew concerned when Hugh called her into their dressing room and said he couldn't remember how to tie his shoes. Jane thought the worst: "Oh my God. He's getting Alzheimer's."

Hugh was equally as anxious. "I couldn't find where we were on the map, which is unusual. I'm very good about maps and directions. I always know where I am. And I was slow. I fell a couple of times over there. The leg just gave way."

The changes in air pressure experienced during the transatlantic flights to and from Italy, probably exacerbated what was an increasingly life-threatening condition. In the clubhouse at Augusta National, while entertaining guests, he collapsed. Clearly, he was a sick man. Doctors in Georgia thought he had the flu and that his condition was exacerbated by dehydration. Fortunately, a friend called another physician who alerted them to another more dire possibility. No one wanted to risk further complications with the fluctuations in air pressure, so rather than a faster return home by air, McColl rode in the back of an ambulance. As it was, the two-and-a-half-hour ride up Interstate 85 to Charlotte was an endurance test of its own. Ambulances are built for stability, not comfort. He felt virtually every bump in the 170-mile journey.

"It was a terrible experience," he recalled. "I thought maybe I was going to die. I wasn't really worried about it. I can't really explain; I was sort of resigned to it. I wasn't fearful. I just thought this was it."

There were more medical consultations in Charlotte before a subdural hematoma was diagnosed. Apparently a small blood vessel in his brain had been damaged when he had fallen on the beach. The family had waited through serious heart bypass surgery five years earlier, but this was far scarier given McColl's medical history and age (seventy-nine). Surgeons drilled holes into his skull to release the buildup of fluid pressing on his brain.

If things went well, then the brain would ease back into place, and McColl would recover. If it shifted too quickly, he could suffer a stroke.

Fortunately, McColl avoided further complications, but he faced a long recovery. A nurse helped him learn to walk again. Once home, his first exercise entailed inching forward with small steps while supporting himself at the six-foot-long island counter in his kitchen. Forward, turn around, return to the other end as a therapist watched closely, ready to catch him should he misstep.

Determined, he graduated from shuffling to and fro in the kitchen to ranging farther into the house, finally developing a circular route. First, he passed through the sitting room where his favorite late nineteenth century painting of America's Cup racers off Newport hangs. From there he moved across to the living room where the walls are filled with more art, then into his booklined office where an old army saber, a gift from noted heart specialist Dr. Francis Robicsek, is stationed over the door—a cozy space, and worthy of a pause, if needed. He'd continue through the foyer and past a short hallway where a Ben Long nude, another favorite, hangs; then through the dining room and back to the kitchen. Every step was measured, and McColl discovered that five times over this circuit equaled a hundred yards. He was told it would take six months for full recovery. He was out of the house within four, but a year passed before he returned to normalcy. Though there was little residual damage, his once purposeful stride was no longer there.

Life changed. He quit drinking. Bottles of expensive single-malt Scotch, most of them presents from good friends who knew his taste for the stuff, went untouched. Unopened bottles remain stashed away with other mementoes in an upper cabinet in his office. He swore off the wine that, before this life-threatening episode, had accompanied both lunch and dinner, with a glass or two in between. He would discover a box full of a favorite vintage six years later while rummaging through personal papers in a storage room. Without alcohol he found he did a lot more listening and less talking at social outings. He laughs knowing that people now believe he doesn't talk much; they have no idea he was called "Motormouth" in college.

Restricted to ground transportation meant he missed quail season at the ranch; a year passed before he headed to Texas again. One morning, he rode as a passenger on a four-wheeler; his shotgun was across his lap. The vehicle flushed a covey, and McColl swung his custom-made Arietta up to his shoulder and dropped a bird, proving that his eye-hand coordination was still what it should be.

During his recovery, Jane found him standing in the kitchen. "Hugh, you know you need to think about this. You've had six bypasses and now a subdural hematoma. You're alive. I think the Lord must have something in store for you. You're supposed to be dead."

Yes, what she said was true. But in the end the experience only made McColl more mindful of the ticking clock as new challenges began moving him in new directions.

He had made good on his promise to the symphony. The underwriting had one more year to run when the 2019–2020 season was cut short by the coronavirus pandemic. The Thrive Campaign had dispersed $7.5 million to other arts organizations, with a balance of $6 million remaining.

Hugh McColl's Texas ranch sits amidst a grove of mesquite and oak trees.

CHAPTER SIX
Home on the Range

H UGH McCOLL'S Texas ranch lies forty-five minutes south of the private airfield at Falfurrias. Railroad tracks across from the gated entrance parallel the right-of-way for U.S. 77. Eighty miles south along that arrow-straight dual-lane highway is Brownsville and the Mexican border's Veterans International Bridge. When McColl's silver Suburban passes through those gates, guarded by flags of the United States and the state of Texas, he enters another world, one that he gleefully touts as a relaxing retreat where ordinary cares don't intrude.

The place McColl considers one of the most beautiful on earth was called the Desert of the Dead when the Spanish ruled this part of North America. Now, it's known as the Wild Horse Desert. The soft sand is covered in wild grasses and other thick vegetation, and the temperatures reach a hundred-plus degrees in the summer. There are dunes fifteen to twenty feet high on the north side of the roughly 40,000 acres that make up McColl's Quail Hunters Heaven, or *Cielo de Cazadores de Codorniz*, but most of the terrain is tabletop flat, with the horizon broken by clumps of mesquite or thickets of scrub oaks called "mottes," short for Spanish "matorral." The wide-open spaces and far horizons have kept McColl coming back over and over again for more than thirty years. He figures that with a schedule of between forty and fifty

A well-armed Hugh McColl posed for a photo to which one wag added the caption, "We don't call 911."

Hugh McColl's house at his Texas ranch, designed by his son John and built by a long-time ranch manager, withstood ninety-mile-per-hour winds of Hurricane Hanna in 2020, suffering only a few leaks in the roof though the storm unroofed ranch buildings and toppled windmills.

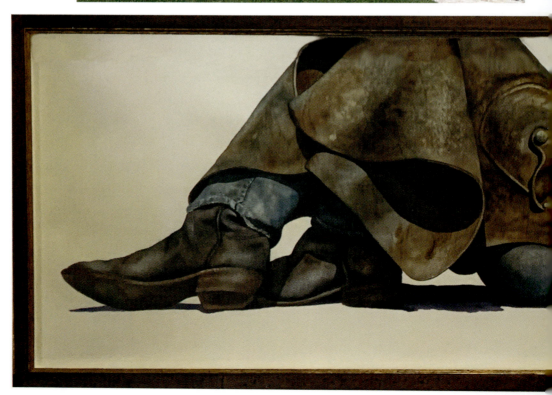

A portrait of Hugh McColl hangs over the mantle, just above a stuffed bobcat.

The main room is a gallery of art and taxidermy, including a numbered Remington sculpture.

One of Hugh McColl's favorite pieces of art is one he posed for. Artist Nelson Boren rendered McColl as a cowboy, his hat pulled down over his eyes, relaxing on his saddle.

days spent hunting each year, he's put in a full four years in South Texas looking for quail and other wild game with a lever-action .30-30 or a double-barrel .20-gauge.

When his life in banking came to a close in 2001, after forty-two years of driving ambition to create the world's most powerful bank, McColl was at loose ends. This was the place where he went to think about what lay ahead. There was no ready answer, and those early years were a little ragged as he wrestled with the changes and varied options. Hugh describes it as a "loveless" time. The ranch helped ease the strain. It's a feel-good place and somewhere McColl can relax and just be a cowboy with a real six-gun on his hip.

Twenty years post retirement, the ranch remains a comfort zone where he is not defined by who he is, or was, back East. There he is an accomplished hunter and fine shot, a cattle man, a generous supporter of community causes, and a good neighbor, if anyone can be really neighborly when living in one of the ten least populated counties in the nation. (The nearest grocery store is a forty-five-minute drive away.)

When he's on the land he dresses casually, wearing T-shirts in black or camouflage, his Levi's cinched with a large custom-made silver ram's head buckle. While he has a variety of ball caps—some read "McColl Camp," and a favorite says "US Marine Corps Veteran"—he also has some wide-brimmed Stetsons. On his feet, he wears snake-guard boots that reach nearly to his knees. He also owns a fancier pair in polished black leather, a gold USMC emblem embossed on the front, full color UNC and NationsBank logos cut into the back, and his initials on the side. These were a gift from President George H.W. Bush after McColl loaned him his plane after Bush's conked out at the Falfurrias airport.

He's well-read in the history of this rough territory that can seem as much Mexican as American. Generations before, the border along the Rio Grande was more a state of mind than anything else. Families migrated back and forth without inhibiting paperwork. That included the forbearers of wellknown bootmaker Armando Duarte Rios whose shop is thirty minutes south of McColl's ranch in Raymondville where the desert sands give way to the rich soil of the Rio Grande Valley. One Saturday morning in late May 2020, Armando greeted McColl with a bear hug as he stepped inside the boot shop. With McColl was a young, newly promoted analyst from Falfurrias Capital. To honor her success in the firm, McColl had Armando fit her for her first pair of custom-made boots. (On this trip, she also fired a gun for the first time, killed a 250-pound hog, and left with the rattles of a five-foot diamondback in her handbag.)

McColl's spread roughly resembles a big square with eight-mile- long sides and lies snug among some of the largest and best-known outfits in Texas. The King ranch is to the north, while the Armstrong ranch, with clout enough to warrant its own U.S. Post Office, is to the south. McColl's leases cover just one part of 235,000 acres owned by a foundation managed by the Catholic Diocese of Corpus Christi. Over the years, McColl's millions in lease payments have gone into funds, secular and nonsecular, that support the church's mission in the region. More Kenedy land lies just to the west and is held in trust, wide open and empty. Hunting is prohibited there; if game makes it through his fence to the other side, it's safe. McColl's hands call it the "Holy Land."

It's deep red Republican territory, as evidenced by the snapshots posted on the bulletin board inside the scruffy office at the landing strip where McColl's NetJets ride touches down after a three-hour flight from Charlotte. The building is about the size of a two-car garage and untamed cactus laps over the concrete entrance. The bulletin board's photo collection includes both presidents Bush, U.S. Senator Mitt Romney, and others from the GOP, including former U.S. Secretary of State James Baker, whose own hunting camp was on land now surrounded by McColl's fences. Former Vice President Richard Cheney had his much-reported hunting accident next door on the Armstrong spread.

Quail Hunters Heaven is an impressive and expensive outlet that costs McColl a small fortune to maintain. At the pit of the Great Recession, which arrived just as the fall hunting season was getting underway in 2008, McColl thought about getting out. The expense was just too much. But the feeling didn't last long. "I'll get over it," he decided. He made some adjustments and ended up in a cost-sharing arrangement with his Falfurrias co-founder, Marc Oken, a longtime hunting companion. Today, Oken's Ghost Camp is within sight of McColl's house and sits just at the edge of a cluster of outbuildings that includes equipment sheds, refrigerated storage for game, a large kennel, and a bunkhouse the guides use during hunting season.

The pursuit of quail provoked McColl's first trip out this way in the mid-eighties. He came with a couple of other Carolinians after the three outbid the competition for a three-day quail hunt on Rio Paisano, a 10,000-acre ranch owned by Frank Horlock of Houston, a millionaire beer distributor. They liked it so much they bought out Horlock's hunting dates for the foreseeable future and then went looking for leased land of their own. McColl eventually ended up with a camp on what's known as the Rita Division, one of three that make up the Kenedy Ranch.

McColl's not the only tenant using the land. Caliche roads crisscross the spread to allow access to the service trucks of an oil and gas company that has punched a number of wells into the Kenedy underground. McColl grumbles about the damage these fracking operations inflict on the landscape by creating piles of spoil and reducing the water table. The hardy roads, made of crushed limestone, do make it easier for him and his crews to get around, but McColl's hunting rigs spend more time off-road, slowly cruising narrow ruts with hunters perched on the rear platform searching for game.

His house lies beyond a grove of mesquite trees, inside a gate guarded by a life-size metal sculpture of a longhorn steer. The compound includes a low-slung "cowboy" house, the ranch manager's house, and a guesthouse that sleeps eight. Designed and built by McColl's son John and a former ranch manager who had a construction background, the compound only came into being after NationsBank board members convinced McColl that a mobile home known for its fleas and flies wasn't a fit place for a man of his stature.

The house's cedar board-and-batten exterior has weathered to a soft gray. Shaded by mesquite trees, its covered front porch is graced by pieces of sculpture—metal representations of cactus—and a half dozen rocking chairs with leather seats and backs. It's a restful spot with ample shade from the mesquite trees and their twisted trunks. The splash of water falling into the tiered bowls on a Florentine fountain eight feet tall covers any spillover sounds from the highway a mile or more away. Just beyond the broad green lawn stands an out-of-service windmill. It used to fill a small pond—in Texas they're called tanks—that attracts wildlife. A feeder dropping corn stands on a slight rise in the distance and attracts turkeys that stroll lazily in for a bite to eat.

The house is divided into two wings, connected by a breezeway. The right side has four hotel-size bedrooms, each with a bath. Well away from the potential disturbance of late-night gatherings, McColl's room is at the far end and boasts a fireplace. His walls are hung with regional artists' work. A few paces outside his door, a Pawleys Island hammock waits, slung between two gnarly trees.

Left of the breezeway, accessed through double doors, is a large room topped by a high, windowed cupola that fills the space with light. Below this hangs a turkey caught midflight, the work of a talented taxidermist. A portrait of McColl, a shotgun balanced on his shoulder, hangs over a huge stone fireplace. A stuffed bobcat poses on the mantle, one large paw draped over the thick, polished slab of mesquite. (McColl thinks the cat wears a permanent expression of arrogance.) Flanking the fireplace, bookshelves are filled with leather-bound Louis L'Amour cowboy novels, books on Texas history, a Spanish-English dictionary, and a deck of "Don't Mess With Texas" playing cards.

Overstuffed leather sofas and two matching wingback chairs are grouped around a low coffee table. On the table sits a numbered copy of a Remington sculpture of a cowboy racing with three longhorns. Beyond this, on the other side of a low wall, a dining table made of heavy mesquite boards can seat ten or more. Nearby, the mounted head of a wild boar flashes its sharp tusks as it guards the wet bar.

The room is a gallery of wildlife art and taxidermy, from feathered quail to the antlered heads of nilgai (pronounced "nail-guy"). This breed of antelope was imported years ago from India onto the King Ranch and thrive in the area despite open season on hunting. The paintings include pieces commissioned by McColl that depict him and a friend raising guns as quail lift into the sky.

You can find Lynn Easley, the ranch's business manager and full-time cook, past the dining room, through a swinging door, in the well-equipped kitchen. Beyond the kitchen is an office and a maid's room. (Lynn was once chief of corporate communications at the bank back in the day. [It's a long story.])

It's a man's camp; Jane travels there only rarely. One winter day, Hugh rang her

> "What in the world am I going to do with him when he can't hunt?"
>
> —Jane McColl

while she was in Naples, Florida, to say the camp cook had just been fired and guests were due soon. Jane didn't take the bait and volunteer to fill in but told him that he had better hire someone quick. She visits on special occasions like Thanksgiving when family members fill the house. There are plenty of good shots among the three generations of McColls as evidenced by a photo of daughter Jane, gun in hand, kneeling beside a dead 300-pound wild boar. (That's his head on the wall.)

The house opened in 1996 with a big party that included an invitation to the bishop in Corpus Christi who negotiates the game leases. Initially, McColl's privileges only covered bobwhite quail, but he subsequently acquired rights for white-tailed deer, turkeys, doves, nilgai, and anything else that runs on four legs or slithers along the ground. (Five- to six-foot-long diamondback rattlers are commonplace.)

The house is solid, anchored by concrete pilings with rebar extending to the rafters. After a storm off the Gulf Coast, less than ten miles east, brought winds at 140 miles per hour, the only damage was the loss of a single shingle. Hurricane Hanna, in July 2020, made a direct hit, and blew roofs off the cowboy camp, toppled windmills and trees, and sent water dripping through leaks in the roof of the main house.

Texans don't always take to easterners, especially those who fly in armed with warrants from the federal government and take over their banks, as McColl did in 1988 when First Republic in Dallas was going under. Some still resent that the Tar Heels used Texas as the launching pad for a nationwide bank. McColl figures there are thousands of people around the state who will never forgive him for the takeover and the debt collections that followed. McColl's pastor, Bob Henderson, while visiting Dallas some years back, mentioned in conversation that McColl was a member of his congregation. Using words wholly unsuited for conversation with a man of the cloth, the man expressed astonishment that McColl had ever set foot in a church.

Henderson assured him that McColl was in church any Sunday when he wasn't in Texas.

Old resentments aside, McColl's neighbors chose him as South Texan of the Year in 2008. The honorees are usually regional figures and include the big-money cattle and oil people whose bona fides go back to the days when Texas had as much in common with Spain as the Carolina colonists did with the King of England. McColl holds this recognition in high regard. It might have had something to do with his deciding not to pack it in when the market turned on him and he considered closing the Texas chapter of his life.

The honors are presented each year at the South Texas Charity Weekend, which includes a celebrity hunt and fund-raising auction. The event coincides with quail season and attracts a crowd that includes politicians, millionaires, and actors such as Larry Hagman and Patrick Duffey from the hit TV show *Dallas*. Attendees arrive

Hugh McColl has hunted game in Texas and beyond, including Spain where he shot pheasant and red-legged partridge with two longtime companions from South Carolina, George Dean Johnson Jr. of Spartanburg (left) and the late E. Craig Wall Jr. of Conway.

with their checkbooks handy, and McColl is known for big purchases, from paintings to guns. His winning bids have sometimes amounted to more than $100,000. One year, after the final item was sold and the organizers were still shy of their goal, McColl bid $4,000 for the auctioneer's vest. Over the years the event has raised more than $15 million for local charities, including wildlife research, the fifty-bed Christus Spohn Hospital-Kleberg in Kingsville, and Halo Flight, the air ambulance service, which has the coordinates of McColl Camp to ensure any injured guests quickly reach the hospital, more than an hour's drive away. Says McColl, "We kind of earned our as hunters, cattle people, participants in everything good."

"This is what I tell people," says Jane. "Hugh is like a child when he gets there. I'm thrilled for him to have the ranch. The only reason I go—I don't hunt. I don't like guns at all. Period. But we go at Thanksgiving and after Christmas and the grandchildren go, so that's fun. I'm thrilled he can still go. I say to people, 'What in the world am I going to do with him when he can't hunt?'" The thought has occurred to her husband as well.

McColl says the hunting is far more exciting than anything he ever found in the Southeast. Back home there's too much ceremony. Things just don't compare. For example, southern hunters often shoot over land salted with farm-raised "released birds." They don't have near the zip of the native quail that dogs flush out of the Texas brush on his ranch. As for other game, there clearly isn't anything like riding a dual-level hunting platform anchored to the back of a Ford 350 as it races across scrub land with the driver dodging gopher holes and hollowed-out sinks while a guide up top keeps his eyes on a slate-blue nilgai bull a hundred yards or more ahead that's fleeing toward the cover of oak treess at thirty miles per hour.

This kind of adrenalin-pumping excitement can challenge even the best shot. In McColl's inventory of occasions to remember is the day he brought down a galloping nilgai with a .45 caliber pistol as his driver moved in close to give him the hope of a clean shot. That was almost as satisfying as the day, a month out from his eighty-fifth birthday, when hunting alongside his grandson, he dropped a nilgai bull at 300 yards with one shot from his favorite Henry lever-action, open-sight .30-30.

While McColl bought the ranch for personal reasons, he put it to use in the deal-making that built Bank of America. In retirement he wondered if the ranch might even produce some income. With the help of Scott Werry, one of the analysts at McColl Partners, he built up a herd of longhorn cattle to about 200 head.

Werry, who grew up on a dairy farm, used what he knew about cattle bloodlines to help McColl select his first herd. This exercise provided more in terms of romantic appeal than it did in financial reward. The cows' hides and horns are where the money is, and the animals tend to live for a very long time. (Victor, the first purchase, still survives, as it were. He went blind and had to be put down. His skull and horns hang over the fireplace on the front porch.)

The occasional sale of hides and horns only modestly offsets expenses. McColl says he's made more selling eighteen-inch square blocks of mesquite—scorched with McColl's brand, CCC (Carolina Cattle Company)—at Erin Vorhoff's trendy shop in Charlotte.

Today, the longhorns make up the smallest portion of a herd of about a thousand head that includes Brahmans and Corrientes, a Spanish breed. Ranch manager Bo Hubert moves the cattle from pasture to pasture to keep the grass under control. Their hooves agitate the ground which helps cultivate seed-producing plants that feed the quail. Hubert also manages a breeding program to produce Angus beef, capitalizing on the fertility and longevity of a mixed breed of Brahman and longhorn cows. The growth of McColl's herd has happily coincided with the changing tastes of American beef eaters, who are willing to pay a premium for steaks cut from grass-fed animals. Cows that once sold for less than a dollar a pound are going for two to two and a half times that.

Among Hubert's other duties is seeing that the game killed on McColl's hunts gets properly processed. The nilgai meat goes to a butcher, where it is prepared into standard cuts and then given to the local food bank. The meat is lean, with a smoother texture than beef. Some of it also makes its way back to the ranch, where Easley uses it in McColl's favorite dish, a variation on an Emeril Lagassé recipe that uses nilgai instead of beef in a brown gravy served over grits.

Hubert calls McColl "Boss" and has the kind of easygoing personality that allows him to tread the fine line between familiarity and fealty. A son of Texas in his early forties, he is strong, tall, and suntanned, with a facility for conversation and cowboy poetry. Hubert and his family live three hours away, near Houston, in the town of El Campo. His wife is a schoolteacher, and his teenage daughter, Samantha, brings home rodeo ribbons in barrel racing competitions. When Hubert was coaching his son Sloan's All-Star baseball team, his family, along with some of the parents and team members traveled to the playoff games in Myrtle Beach, South Carolina, on McColl's plane. The boss also saw to it that the Huberts and their friends had a similarly nice ride to the national rodeo finals in Las Vegas.

Hubert knows the land and can read the signs left by the passing parade of wild game. During hunting season, he serves as guide, using subtle hand signals and a slight whistle to communicate with the driver of the Ford 350 so shooters can line up a good shot.

He can also spot evidence of migrants on their way north after crossing the border. When drivers bringing carloads up the highway reach the ranch's southern boundary, the doors open and the "illegals," as Hubert calls them, move into the bush to walk overland, trying to avoid the U.S. Border Patrol checking station on U.S. 77 just north of the ranch entrance. All through traffic must stop for inspection there and the station is well manned with cameras, dogs, and guns. The migrants' attempts to bypass the station have produced unfortunate and fatal results in this part of Texas for years.

Bodies and bones found over the years on the Kenedy lands are reminders of why this was once called the Desert of the Dead. Many who make the effort don't have sufficient water or proper clothing, especially footwear. It's dangerous on the ground—hence McColl's tall boots. Even the deceptive branches of the low-growing tasajillo cactus have tiny barbs that can sink into the skin of passersby and cause serious infections. While the soft sand and grasses are easy enough to look at, a simple walk across even flat land can turn into hard labor. People die. Hubert was once on a tractor pulling a disc harrow to cultivate a crop of goatweed, a favorite feed for quail, when he came across human bones. They had been there for a long time, so it was hard to determine time of death. The authorities were called nonetheless.

The nagging issue of immigration, the volatile politics of Donald Trump, and the general red nature of local politics is different than McColl's brand which is decidedly bluer than that of his Texas neighbors, most of whom have been putting Republicans in office for years. But it's not hard to avoid touchy subjects, he says. Out there folks are more interested in the price of cattle, the price of oil, "and if the quail crop is good." He explains, "They could care less about the Russians or anybody." He does know that the border has been porous for many years, and changes to that complicate the farming and ranching life in this part of Texas. Trump's wall is not popular. For himself, he is sympathetic to those entering illegally and putting their lives at risk trying to cross miles of hostile territory on foot where rattlesnakes are likely assassins. "We have trucks to get around," he says. "They are walking."

Lively conversation is what makes the ranch appealing to McColl. The large fireplace on the porch is his version of late-night TV. He selects his guests with an awareness of their interest in hunting but also the capacity to carry on thoughtful conversation when things get dull riding through the brush. On his pastor's first visit, McColl brought along an evangelical Christian and a medical doctor to round out the party. Said Bob Henderson, "There was some discussion about religion, but we had some rigorous discussions about the modern-day situation of health care."

McColl and Henderson also dug into the subject of immigration on that visit. Henderson remembers: "It was fascinating to see how he balanced his convictions with following the law. I thought he did a remarkable job on that. At the edge of his property he has a well that has a Catholic shrine on it from the local Catholic monastery. Local priests came out to bless it, so word spread of its location at the very edge of his property. Anybody needing water along a worn traffic pattern of immigration can reach it.

"That was his recognizing the dignity of human beings and operating within the confines of the law. One time—he wouldn't mind me saying this now—we were hunting, and we've got these two trucks, and we're like a rolling arsenal. We have every rifle known to humankind, and we're out on a 40,000-acre ranch where nobody knows anything, and we saw an immigrant group going by. They're scared to death. We're armed. They're out in the middle of the desert. They're undocumented.

"We went up to them and they asked the quickest way to the highway, and we pointed them in that direction, and then we later reported them. We don't know what happened. I thought that was another kind of fascinating balance of 'I'm going to recognize human dignity and the desperation of these people, and I'm going to follow the laws of our country and do the right thing and let it work out.'"

McColl's current lease is good through 2024, and he jokes with his people out west that he's going to be sure to live until the lease runs out. That would put him at an expiration date of eighty-nine. That's too young, so he's thinking about at least one more five-year option.

Chapter Seven
Son of the South

A QUIET, EVEN somber, mood had settled over the concert hall on that Friday afternoon in mid-September 2016 by the time Hugh McColl stepped out to speak. The free midday performance of the Charlotte Symphony Orchestra was billed as a "Concert for Peace" and followed nights of protests after the death of Keith Lamont Scott, an African American man shot by police. Though businesses in Uptown, including McColl's bank, had closed for the day, he refused to show the white feather to the disruption and had gone to his office that morning. When he got a call asking him to attend the concert and say a few words, he accepted immediately.

"The time is now. I challenge everyone, particularly the white community, to begin today to talk and listen to the concerns of each other," a newspaper reporter quoted him telling the several hundred or so seated in the Belk Theater. As Maestro Christopher Warren-Green prepared to raise his baton, McColl concluded, "Black lives do matter. It's time to come together to solve our social and economic problems. The main thing we need to do is start talking with each other, not past each other."

McColl had been traveling out of state, but had seen televised images of roving protestors in the hours after the shooting. Police cars had been damaged, and the noisy and unruly crowd eventually pushed onto Interstate 85, bringing traffic to a halt. Drivers were threatened, and goods in one tractor trailer were dragged to the roadway and set afire. Further protests and confrontations with police continued the following night on Uptown streets. With the turmoil shrouded in clouds of tear gas, another man was shot and later died at the hospital.

By the time McColl returned to Charlotte, the city's image was not gleaming office towers, but a tall, athletic Black man with dreadlocks. Stripped to the waist, his jeans slung low, he stood with his left fist raised before a line of helmeted police officers. This picture appeared on screens all around the country, through multiple news cycles, and even drew comment from the White House. By the time of the Friday afternoon concert, the National Guard was in the city and ready to patrol Charlotte's streets for the first time since 1968 in the aftermath following the assassination of the Rev. Dr. Martin Luther King Jr. McColl, deeply unsettled, resolved to do something.

This wasn't the first cloud to cast shade on Charlotte's carefully cultivated vision as a place of twenty-first-century opportunity, progress, and growth. Recently published studies had presented a stark contrast between rich and poor; Charlotte had more wealthy households than elsewhere in the state, but four of North Carolina's ten most disadvantaged census tracts could be found there, too. One was in the part of town where police shot Scott that September afternoon. Also weighing on the community was another study that revealed children in Charlotte born in poverty were unlikely to ever rise out of it. Charlotte's prospects of upward mobility were the lowest of the nation's fifty largest cities.

"A racialized, concentrating poverty has led to the creation of some of North Carolina's most intense pockets of economic distress in the state's most commercially vibrant and successful city." That was University of North Carolina law professor Gene Nichol's assessment of the city in his book, *The Faces of Poverty in North Carolina*.

Less than a month after the protests, McColl found himself with former mayor Harvey Gantt at another forum on leadership and the city's welfare. In the audience were members of the upper echelon of the Charlotte business community. McColl and Gantt talked for nearly two hours and received a standing ovation at the end. During that time, McColl repeated much of what he had said many times before. Charlotte's problems weren't new. Racial division, economic inequality, and public schools that had racially re-segregated over the previous ten years, after the essence of the *Swann* case had been set aside by the Court, were serious problems and impediments to the city's future. "If we just mouth platitudes and think everything is going to be fine, it's not," McColl said that day. "It can't be our way of doing things." He spoke of inequality in jobs and incomes and being able to find decent places to live. "We're dealing with prejudice that takes the form of not caring."

Turning the attention of his fellow citizens toward Charlotte's social and economic health has been on McColl's agenda for decades. He delivered a version of his 2016 remarks at a virtually identical gathering twenty-five years earlier. In 1991, speaking at a Chamber retreat in Pinehurst, he assessed Charlotte this way: "To outsiders, our city appears to prosper. And by many measurements, it has. While we have scored many gains, we have lost even more.

"We have lost sensitivity to the 'have-nots'; we have lost our sensitivity to people of other races. We have lost a common purpose and divided ourselves into groups who are only against things and not for things."

Over the years, McColl has been both Charlotte's proudest promoter and champion on the one hand and, on the other, the public figure most likely to highlight the city's social problems. "We talked about banking when we had to," his former speechwriter, John Cleghorn, said, but the topics that engaged McColl most ranged broadly from raising his children to raising cities where families could enjoy a decent life. The soul of McColl's corporation was what attracted Cleghorn to NCNB in 1990 and kept him there for seventeen years. During that time, he helped McColl find opportunities to speak to audiences at national gatherings of organizations like the Urban League and the NAACP where his boss often drew attention to the needs of cities or made the case for minority business development and fair treatment in the workplace. Said Cleghorn: "He was progressive but not a bleeding heart."

McColl was on the downslope of his chairmanship at Bank of America when he ruminated with a friend about how he would use his remaining time. Talking about the inequalities in society and the people left behind, he thought, would be a good use of his energy and his position. "I think I have an opportunity yet to do some things … in the area of race. I have the platform with this huge powerful machine [that gives me] a bully pulpit to stand up and talk about some hard issues that we keep ignoring here in the South and we ignore in America."

"You could argue," he continued, "that in the South, the educated class of people have had an inordinate growth over the last thirty years in terms of their personal incomes and their style of living, and standard of living and everything else. And we had left a lot of people behind. And I think I have a platform in which I can talk about that, and what needs to be done."

In the months prior to the 2016 demonstrations on Charlotte's streets, McColl had resolved to renew those earlier impulses. At the time he was acutely aware that a different outcome of the surgery for his subdural hematoma could have left him virtually speechless and disabled. Going forward, he planned to deal more intentionally with the consequences of racial and economic inequality and the damage it inflicted on his city. It was not the usual or necessary preoccupation of a wealthy eighty-year-old. His reputation was secure, he was not seeking public office or approval, he was very comfortable in his own skin. Yet, it was the choice of a man who was keen enough to recognize that his generation had an obligation to set some things right, to recognize that there were unfinished tasks. And he would begin with himself and the prejudices that inhabited his own soul.

Born in 1935, McColl grew up in the Jim Crow South. He spent his childhood in a home with a spacious veranda, surrounded by graceful gardens that enjoyed a wide reputation, and with enough African American servants to take care of every household need. His family hadn't settled the town of Bennettsville, South Carolina, but his great-grandfather, Duncan D. McColl, had certainly ushered it into the twentieth century by providing ample supplies of capital and enterprise. There was the bank that he had helped organize in 1884, the railroad he had built, and the cotton mills that processed the bounty produced on McColl land. He came from a lineage of proud Scotsmen, the third Hugh Leon McColl, and the second named Hugh Jr. at birth, in as many generations.

The McColl family compound was roughly three square blocks—nine acres in all—of family homes, some offices, and a Baptist church built from the largesse of the family. His mother, Frances, a college-educated artist, read classic novels to Hugh and his siblings—an older sister whom he adored and two younger brothers. She managed a household set in a turreted Victorian home that was really never her own. She and Hugh's father had moved in with his parents after they married in 1929. Her mother-in-law, widowed two years later, remained an elegant, commanding presence in the family for the first thirty-plus years of Frances's married life.

Tens of thousands of irises filled Gabrielle Drake McColl's Green Gate Garden. This was no idle enterprise. The garden featured two hundred fifty varieties and produced enough rhizomes to support a mail-order business with a catalog of a dozen pages. Prices for a single cutting ranged from a few cents to as much as a working man might earn in a month.

"We're dealing with prejudice that takes the form of not caring."

—Hugh McColl

Hugh's father was a quiet, serious man sobered by the responsibilities of assuming control, at the age of twenty-six, of the family business interests after his own father's fatal heart attack in 1931. It took a few years, but even with the burden of the Great Depression, he perfected an orderly closure of the family-owned Bank of Marlboro, returned money to depositors, and distributed the balance to shareholders. He never envied another man, his son is fond of saying, and never told a dirty joke or laughed at one. "Frugal" doesn't adequately describe his tidy habits. He spent his life overseeing the family business interests, tied mostly to cotton, as both a broker and a grower. In addition, he managed a conservative portfolio of investments.

Racial segregation may have been morally indefensible and wholly inconsistent with the U.S. Constitution, but it was considered neither extraordinary nor strange in its time. It just was. In the McColl household Black servants cooked the meals and served tea to Gabrielle and her friends when they gathered in the parlor in the afternoon. They cleaned the house, did the laundry, tended the garden, and at least two women looked after the four children from their earliest days until they reached puberty. The Hugh McColl Jr. born in 1935 grew up taking this arrangement for granted but never saw it for what it was until he was well into adulthood. He would later remember with deep regret that he never acknowledged the devotion of the nurse named Anna who cared for him as a child. He last saw her in the late 1950s when he was just home from the Marine Corps, his pockets full of poker winnings. "She was poor," he remembers. "I now realize very poor. It's always bothered me that I didn't give her any money." She died not long after.

There was some interplay of the races on the ball fields behind the McColl home inside the family compound. When the McColl brothers got to organizing a baseball team, the two sides had to include boys from the neighborhood or there was no game. Down at the McColl place on Jennings Street, on Bennettsville's west side, that meant poor whites and Blacks. Most all of the town's wealthy white citizens lived on the east side, where the newer twentieth-century development had taken place. As Hugh grew older, he came to know the fieldworkers who rode the labor bus he began driving at the age of fourteen and the Black farmers whose cotton he checked off when they brought it to the family-owned gin to be weighed and processed. The older men trusted the youngster, who was already using the double-entry bookkeeping he learned from his father. He held his own with adults. Supremely self-assured even as a teenager, he traveled alone by train from Bennettsville to New York City to see Joe DiMaggio and the New York Yankees defeat the Brooklyn Dodgers in the 1949 World Series.

McColl remembers Bennettsville as a "sundown town," one of those communities where the movements of Blacks were restricted in the evening hours and a nightly siren signaled Blacks to return east of Broad Street, the main thoroughfare that dissected the heart of town. Marian Wright Edelman grew up there, too. Edelman's father, the Reverend Arthur Jerome Wright, was the minister at Shiloh Baptist Church, within shouting distance of the McColl compound. The two would not meet until they were adults, in their fifties, yet when she was a child in the 1940s, she walked by his house almost daily on her way to Marlboro Training High School, the center of education for African Americans of all grades.

Edelman, four years younger than McColl, would graduate from Spelman College, study at the Sorbonne in Paris, earn a law degree at Yale, and figure prominently in the civil rights movement in the 1960s. In 1973, she founded the Children's Defense Fund, a national advocacy organization paying particular attention to the needs of children of color, the poor, and the disabled. Like McColl, she was raised by adults who prepared her for a demanding future by administering generous doses of confidence. She was encouraged to read and express herself at an early age and lived in a world that was remarkably expansive and fertile. The president of Atlanta's Morehouse College was a guest in her home. So was the celebrated Black educator Mary McLeod Bethune. By a quirk of timing, the African American poet Langston Hughes arrived unexpectedly one day and ended up giving a reading at her school.

Edelman's everyday world reached from her father's church to the row of Black-owned business one block off Bennettsville's main drag. The area was called "the Gulf," a name borrowed from a filling station that had once occupied one corner of a nearby intersection. Along those few blocks, just behind the county jail, were a string of businesses including a restaurant, a barbershop, a pool hall, a drugstore, and the Palace, a movie theater that somehow got the popular Westerns before the one patronized by whites. Today, Bennettsville's public library, a handsome twenty-first-century building that Hugh McColl helped pay for, is named in Edelman's honor. In the days of Jim Crow, the library was off-limits for Black patrons like her, as was the water fountain in the Belk department store, where a sign above it read "White."

In the spring of 1954, McColl was nearing the end of his freshman year at the University of North Carolina in Chapel Hill when, back in Bennettsville, Edelman was a teenager eagerly waiting, along with her father, for news from the U.S. Supreme Court, whose justices were writing a decision in a case called *Brown v. Board of Education*. They were well aware that the case included a lawsuit that challenged segregated schools in South Carolina. Edelman and her father, part of the crowd gathered at the Marlboro County Courthouse, heard South Carolina governor James F. Byrnes declare that Bennettsville would never see Black children and white children sit together in public school classrooms. Nonetheless, Reverend Wright waited hopefully, searching for news about the Court and its deliberations in the pages of the *Pittsburgh Courier* and the *Baltimore Afro-American*, two Black-owned papers that circulated in the South. Wright never got to share with his daughter in the joyful relief that African Americans experienced on hearing of the Court's ruling outlawing segregation. He died the week before the landmark opinion was read aloud by Chief Justice Earl

Warren on May 17, 1954.

That day in 1954 left an indelible imprint on a young Black teenager; it passed with little notice for McColl. "So you grew up with racism," he reflected many years later. "You didn't know that's what it was. I don't think I was aware of it. I always said the worst thing about me as a racist was that I never thought it was a problem. Inequality didn't bother me as a child or as a teenager and maybe even as a college student. It was all around me, but it was a state of normalcy."

> " The worst thing about me as a racist was that I never thought it was a problem."
> —Hugh McColl

McColl finally met Edelman in 1991, when he was invited to her home in Washington D.C., to meet the Children's Defense Fund board of directors who were honoring CDF's chair, Hillary Rodham Clinton. At the time, Clinton's husband, Arkansas governor, Bill Clinton, was running for president. McColl chatted with Clinton, but he found Edelman and the opportunity to connect over their early parallel lives in Bennettsville more engaging. She was inspired by his bank's ranking among large U.S. corporations as the best place to work for women and working mothers. Because NCNB had recently made news by promising an investment of $10 billion in lending to low- and moderate-income borrowers, Edelman put McColl on the program for CDF's annual meeting the following year in Atlanta.

By the early 1990s, McColl had made significant changes in the bank's culture with policies that equalized opportunity for all employees, whether they were women, gay, or Black; his reputation for acquiring banks largely overshadowed the institution's social impact. Provisions for day care, diversity in hiring, and expanding business for minority vendors rarely made it into the articles about his ambition to create a regional financial powerhouse. Writers would have discovered the breadth of McColl's commitment if they had talked to Ron Leeper, a Black man ten years his junior. The two had met in the late 1970s when restive racial politics shifted the power of the Charlotte City Council. Newly adopted district representation opened the election process to outliers like Leeper, who provided McColl with a new perspective on the city he thought he knew well.

In 1977, Leeper, thirty-two, bearded and with a four-inch afro, was a member of the Black Panther Party. (Forty-plus years later, his facial hair was reduced to an almost imperceptible pencil mustache.) His job as district manager at a wholesale supply company produced a paycheck and not a whole lot more. His first brush with politics was organizing a homeowners' association in his neighborhood. He subsequently joined the petition campaign that brought district representation to the city council. At his first opportunity, he filed as a candidate in one of the new districts. Half of the voters were white, and about half were Black. He won.

At the time, McColl was taking his first steps with the bank to revive downtown Charlotte's Fourth Ward with a vision that saw beyond the trash-filled vacant lots, the abandoned homes, and the dilapidated buildings with reputations as shot houses or worse. McColl's intended future might be called gentrification—not considered a bad thing at the time. Leeper, however, had more immediate concerns. His West Charlotte district was plagued with an overabundance of public housing and municipal neglect. If the nation's Midwest was flyover country, West Charlotte was drive-through country for downtown executives like McColl who were in a hurry to reach the airport. Driving West Boulevard to the NCNB hangar, McColl was mindful of jaywalking pedestrians, but he was largely unaware of the urban blight that surrounded him on the way.

McColl was eager to meet the new people that redistricting brought to the council, so he put in a call to Leeper. The city's establishment, which had enjoyed support from the old crowd, most of whom came from the well-to-do white precincts, would need the support of these new folk if they were to get money needed for such things as airport expansion and center-city development. Leeper's to-do list was more personal. "These new council members were talking a little different language than what McColl was accustomed to hearing," he recalled. "I probably was the most extreme on that. I'm not sure that he ever ran into anybody who said, 'I'm not going to support things you want if you're not going to support things that I want.'"

In one of their early meetings, Leeper told McColl about streets in his district lined with sorry rental houses where the refuse, such as old furniture and mattresses left behind by evicted tenants, went uncollected by the sanitation department. He told him about drug dealers doing business with impunity. At one point, McColl recalled, Leeper told him something about open sewers, and that's when he said, "Enough. Show me." Leeper chauffeured McColl around streets in his district replete with examples of willful neglect by those charged with making the city livable. McColl then backstopped Leeper's complaints to city hall, and the refuse disappeared. Violators of the sanitation code were brought to heel, and police patrols improved. All the while, Leeper was growing more receptive to what McColl wanted from city hall. Their lunch meetings became a monthly occurrence.

No topic was off the table, including the touchy business of NCNB's investment in South Africa, whose apartheid government made it the pariah among nations. McColl was the one responsible for putting the bank's money behind innovative lending and leasing projects abroad. That made the complaints personal when picketers showed up outside NCNB's headquarters and activist shareholders demanded NCNB divest and leave immediately. At the time, South African lending made up as much as half of the bank's international portfolio, and McColl did not endear himself to the community when he was quoted as saying apartheid had never killed anyone.

Leeper recalled picking his way through the demonstrators one day on his way to McColl's office and their monthly lunch. Over sandwiches, the subject turned to South Africa, and Leeper challenged McColl's point of view. At one point, McColl rose and walked to his window and looked down to the plaza area at the bank's front door. "You know, I know those people down there," McColl told him. "They're down there with signs calling Hugh McColl a racist and accusing the bank of perpetuating racism. The thing I like about you most is that even though you and I have issues, you are always willing to talk and listen. It bothers me that some of those people down there know me the same way, but they didn't ask for a meeting. They just got their posters and signs and started calling me a racist."

McColl was not ignorant of conditions in South Africa. He had traveled there several times, and his curiosity was never in check. Bill Vandiver of the bank's international division said one trip included the customary calls on customers, and even the head of the government, but McColl also made it a point to seek out leaders of the political opposition, including prominent churchmen and others who had been jailed multiple times for protesting racist government policies. One day, Vandiver heard McColl tell their driver to head to Soweto, the huge Black enclave outside of Johannesburg, where McColl kept directing the driver to go deeper and deeper into the township where some of the poorest people lived. "We [stopped and] went into a woman's house, dirt floor and all of that," Vandiver recalled, "and he sat there and talked to the lady. The driver was absolutely petrified. He thought he was going to get executed. But that's the kind of information McColl wanted."

The talks with the dissidents, the stop in Soweto, the general mood of the country added up to one thing for McColl: apartheid would not last. The mixture of politics and business didn't resonate then as it would later. "We stayed until we were ordered out by our government. We never lost a dime down there, and we did a lot of good," he would later recall. "We gave a lot of money to charities, and we helped furnish a lot of jobs."

The South African rant was at its loudest as McColl and NCNB turned to the Third Ward, another sad area of the center city. Fourth Ward produced a neighborhood of mainly upper-middle-class whites and Blacks who could afford the gamble. Move-in costs for new homes and rehabbed period structures were high. Across town, in Third Ward, McColl wanted homes and apartments at affordable prices that would allow residents to continue to live there after the overhaul was complete. McColl grew impatient when the bank's man on the job reminded him of the racial bias that Charlotte Realtors faced when marketing homes in what was largely an African American part of town. "We're making a lot of money in South Africa, and we jolly well ought to be doing something good for the people in our own community," the late Dennis Rash said McColl told him one day. "He was motivated to do the same in First Ward, too. Our efforts to build affordable housing weren't mandated [by the government]. That was just what you ought to do in order to be fair."

McColl really took a liking to Leeper's fellow council member Harvey Gantt. Gantt, an architect, had gained national attention in the mid-1960s when he broke the color barrier at Clemson University in South Carolina. Gantt and McColl shared a common desire to develop the center city along the lines of a master plan prepared in 1966 by A. G. Odell, Gantt's first boss and mentor. Covering virtually all the land that would later lie inside the Interstate 277 loop, Odell's plan remained relevant a half-century later. He envisioned high-rise apartments, a sports stadium in the center city, and shopping and dining within walking distance of one's home and place of work. Today, Odell is long gone, but his vision stands. More than 30,000 people live in high-rise apartments in Uptown Charlotte that overlook Bank of America Stadium. Restaurants and nightspots abound.

Gantt designed two of the first homes in Fourth Ward; one for his family and the other for his friend, Mel Watt, who was later elected to Congress. When Gantt announced his candidacy for mayor in 1983, McColl issued a fulsome endorsement, which at the time was considered a mark of political courage. McColl's support wasn't well received even though two decades had passed since the passage of the Voting Rights Act. In response, the top executive at one of NCNB's large corporate customers closed his company's account and sold his stock, angry that McColl would lend his, and by association the bank's, name to a Black politician. (McColl recalls with some satisfaction that this fit of pique, coming at a time when the bank's stock was in a slump, ultimately cost the man $20 million when the share price recovered.) There were other slights and slurs. McColl suspected one of his neighbors of stuffing his mailbox with a copy of the sheet music to "Darktown Strutters Ball" and an election night photo of McColl and Gantt. Word also got back to him that some considered his endorsement of Gantt to be insincere, claiming he was only trying to promote the bank among African Americans.

The cynics missed the point. McColl had never pandered to any one slice of society. His aggressive commitment to a culture of meritocracy meant that every employee had a chance to succeed. Beginning in the 1980s and continuing for decades, McColl stripped away the vestiges of discrimination that had limited the advancement of women and African Americans. If a teammate publicly disclosed his or her sexual orientation during what was a difficult era for gays, McColl paid it no mind. If any of his subordinates objected, they did so at risk to their careers.

McColl often raised the topic of diversity and made clear to the officers of the banks that were acquired by NCNB, and later NationsBank, just what that meant.

John Cleghorn accompanied McColl to St. Louis in 1996 for a speech and introductory appearance before the top two tiers of management at Boatman's Bancshares. At the conclusion of McColl's usual team-building remarks for newly acquired properties, Cleghorn said McColl "looked out on them and said, 'This room doesn't have enough people of color in it. When I come back next year that had better have changed.' He was very clear about that. He wasn't saying that just to be heard. There wasn't anybody in that room he had to kowtow to. He meant it." Before McColl retired, an African American named Ed Dolby was running the bank's operations in the Carolinas and Virginia.

As Hugh McColl was wrapping up his career in banking in 2001, Sy Pugh was sixty miles south on Interstate 85 playing basketball and later coaching at Limestone College, a nondenominational Christian school in Gaffney, South Carolina. Standing six nine, twelve inches taller than McColl, he is well captured by McColl's offhand description of him as "someone who could go bear hunting with a switch." That's just the start of the comparisons between the two. Pugh, who arrived in Charlotte in 2003, is Black and roughly half McColl's age. Both are Christians, al-

He's done so much for the city in so many different ways, but he still feels like he hasn't done enough.

To me that's inspirational."

—SY PUGH

though McColl is more of a pray-in-the-closet Presbyterian, while Pugh teaches a Bible study class at a nondenominational congregation populated by several thousand evangelicals. Despite the differences, they have sustained an open, engaging friendship that energizes a biracial breakfast club called the Champions. Since 2017, forty to fifty men have met monthly to consider delicate questions of race and culture.

The Champions grew out of a loosely organized gathering of whites and Blacks, assembled largely by word of mouth, several months after Keith Lamont Scott's death. Those attending represented a variety of backgrounds, ages, and professions, but all agreed to deal straight and openly with one another on touchy topics. McColl was encouraged to take part by a longtime community leader and friend who knew him from church. She was aware racial inequity had long been on his agenda and that growing old had not relieved him of an obligation to deal with it. "One of the problems in America," McColl said, "is we don't allow ourselves to see the things that are distasteful about our society or we make up some defense of it that seems logical but isn't. I'm not trying to change society; I really just do my thing."

Pugh remembers the first time he sat down to talk with McColl about the Champions. The two were at a conference table in a suite of offices where Pugh runs the operations side of an investment firm. "He was sitting right there where you are sitting and said he didn't feel like he had done enough. I am thinking, This is Hugh McColl. He's done so much for the city in so many different ways, but he still feels like he hasn't done enough. To me, that's inspirational."

For McColl, he was merely displaying the foundational element to building trust: being willing to tell the truth. When he was at his bank, mutual trust was the code of the company. "It is a very simple philosophy," he says. "It is taking people, everybody, at face value, and saying, 'Hey, come aboard, let's go.' It works. All people like the environment of trust where you can speak up and say what you think and not be crucified for it."

From the outset, McColl compiled a record of faithful attendance at Champions meetings, even during hunting season. There is no mistaking that his presence boosted participation, says Pugh. Having someone of his stature gave the meetings heft and substance. McColl was committed. "Sy and I both see it as a place where we come together to get to know each other as men and get beyond race and cultural differences while trying to find the things we have in common and wanting to respect each other.

And I guess everybody there thinks they're doing that." He continued, "And one of the things we've asked all the white people to do is to face up to their own prejudices. Everybody will tell you that they are not prejudiced. Almost every white man you talk to will tell you, 'I don't have any prejudice.' And then they'll say something like they treat everybody the same or something. But implicit in every statement of course is the racist thought that A, we tolerate somebody, or B, we give them equality with us. So it all starts from a premise of being better, whether you know it or not. So it's a little bit like going to confession.

"Now, what we've learned is all of us have racist thoughts that come unsummoned. And the reason we have them is we learned them when we were six years old, or four years old, or five years old. Like [when] I grew up, Blacks were in their place, so to speak, and everybody thought it was normal."

Those new to McColl's company come away with an appreciation of his candor and, as more than one person put it, his "authenticity." One of those is Dionne Nelson, a successful for-profit developer of housing in mixed-income neighborhoods. Like McColl, she was raised in South Carolina. In 2019, the offices of her company, Laurel Street, were in a refurbished early twenties home in Charlotte's Dilworth neighborhood, but her associates were working on plans to move to a location with more space. Nelson was in an audience one day when McColl had the floor and the subject turned to race. They were acquaintances, but still some time away from his becoming an investor in her company. She listened closely while he shared his reaction upon hearing that a talented African American woman with an MBA from Harvard was running a successful business building affordable housing in Charlotte. He said, "The first thought that flashed through my head was that she must have had some help."

"And I'm in the room," Nelson said. "He didn't use my name, but I presume it's me, and there was a part of me that was hurt, but there was also a part of me knowing how the story ends. That part speaks volumes about his ability to be open-minded and see past his own bias and go completely to the opposite end of the spectrum. So he started out with a hesitation or doubt about me and ended up as an investor. That tells me a lot about who he is, and it probably says a lot about the ability of how and why he's as successful as he is."

McColl's public conversation about race is not for show, Nelson discovered. He opens up to others and expects them to do the same. Offering personal experiences is a way of gaining trust with those for whom trust is in limited supply. McColl surprised her one day when he began telling her the story of his childhood nurse. "Like, why is he telling me that?" she remembers. "I don't know what he intended, but what it told me [was] he does have a comfort around people of color that allows him to, I think, to see something different. And that is refreshing. But I think the more powerful piece is, again, you don't just think about it, you actually do something with it.

"I mean, he is of a generation where a white man would not have felt like he owed anything to some Black woman that was a servant in his home," she said. "So if he's carrying that 'I should have done more,' that says something about a caring for people, all people. That's pretty powerful. The fact that he's challenged himself on the choices he's made over the years, that he's chosen to say, 'Well, the next time I get an opportunity to make a difference, I'm going to make a difference,' says something about his integrity."

McColl feels a connection with those who face discrimination. He admits that he can't possibly understand how racism affects African Americans because whites "have never been insulted or treated with disdain because of our color." He explains: "We are not able to put ourselves in a Black person's place. Although I've felt some of the prejudice, unwarranted prejudice." To that point, McColl recalls salient elements in his own story. He's short and a southerner; both have produced personal slights in his past. The former turned him into a pugnacious competitor beginning when he was a lad. The latter often meant strangers immediately discounted his intelligence. "'He's from the South. He must be dumb.' That drove me to retaliate and build a company that was bigger and tougher than any of them," he says.

A Black friend once told McColl that being Black was like moving furniture around a room for a wife who couldn't quite make up her mind: "You have to carry the chair from here to there, but you don't get to put it down. When you're Black, you can't put down the chair. You're always Black. Every time somebody looks at you, they see Black, and you know they see something that they impute to you, which may be an inferior intelligence, et cetera, that you can't get rid of."

After several years of Champions meetings McColl's enthusiasm for the process began to flag. He found himself questioning the investment of time. He was disappointed in the relative silence of those closest to his age, who didn't participate as he thought they should. At the same time, he recognized that this older cohort were the ones who grew up in an era when a frank exchange between whites and Blacks was generally discouraged or avoided as much as possible. Speaking up could have consequences. It didn't come easily to them, even in the safe environment created by the group. "The real issue for all of us is where do we go from here," McColl said. "We can't fix yesterday; we just cannot fix it. There's nothing that can be changed. I haven't figured out what to do with all this yet."

Pugh says the real measure of the program is how men use it outside the group. "My challenge is always, what are you doing with it personally? Are you taking it back to your personal circle and using it there? So it's one thing to come together in this group, we can pretend to be authentic right here. But if I saw you out with your friends, would I be welcome if it's someone that does not look like me? I think guys are showing up, at least that's what they're saying. They're coming because there's work that they need to do. They're coming to say, 'How can I help someone else as well?' It's really become a twofold thing. I think anything I'm a part of, it's got to be a reciprocal relationship."

McColl loves history. He can reel off the names and reputations of centuries of McColls, including a rebellious lot who lived in the Scotland highlands four hundred years ago. The lessons of political upheavals, whether they are provoked by social or political unrest, are not lost on him, and he believes America's running perilously close to revolution at the present time. The tipping point could easily be race. Whites, especially older whites like him, find themselves in a society they don't recognize. The norms provided by the comfortable majority status they have known all their lives is slipping away and will soon disappear. America will have a society shared among those who are white, Black, and brown.

"What we are seeing in the United States is the death rattle of the white male power structure," McColl says. "All this Trump following is really white males that feel their power going away to women and to Blacks and to Asians. But it's over, because the population mix is permanently altered.

"Most of our people really don't get it. They know that things are changing, and they don't really like it. Nobody likes change. Trump's 'Make America Great Again' really means 'Make It White Again,' and he can't do that. We're already a polyglot nation, and whether it's good, bad, or indifferent, it doesn't matter. We may go through several upheavals, even gunfire, before it's over. I'll be long dead, but it's going to happen. We're struggling with it. We don't know how to deal with it.

"The issue that I think we're all still dealing with is you can't clean the slate. Black people have a hard time forgiving insults, which have been heaped upon them for four hundred years. The young Blacks haven't really had to put up with what the older Blacks had to put up with. They are impatient and not going to put up with any crap. I see and hear a difference between the older ones and the younger ones and just how they react. Healing is difficult."

McColl and Bob Henderson, his minister at Covenant Presbyterian, have spent time on the subject of race in the evenings sitting before the fire in Texas. "I think he sees the potential for real, structural social problems for our country if we don't get at rectifying some of the disparity that's expressed largely across racial lines," Henderson says. "So he sees a huge wealth gap as a real social problem. I think he understands that when societies endure that for long, they resolve it by revolution, and he would like to work towards a better way."

McColl's efforts to engage people in dialogue about race go beyond the Champions breakfasts. One of the numbers stored in his phone belongs to Braxton Winston. He is the tall, lanky Black man whose defiant raised fist became the iconic image of the 2016 protests. Their paths crossed in 2017 at a gathering that led to the launch of the Champions sessions. That evening Winston was harshly questioning Charlotte's police chief, Kerr Putney. In the weeks following the protests, Winston had repeatedly called for the chief's resignation. Winston arrived at the meeting fresh from a district court appearance where misdemeanor charges stemming from his participation in a street protest had been dismissed. Though some might have said he appeared angry, Pugh described Winston as brimming with "unbridled passion."

During Winston's exchange with the chief, McColl raised a question about the uneasy relations between the police and African Americans. Why didn't Charlotte's Black citizens trust the police? McColl's query brought Winston up short. "In a certain group of people, the question might not have ever gotten thought about or answered, but I thought it was legitimate," Winston recalled. "When he asked that, I was kind of like, Hm, he's really thinking about stuff. And he was approachable in the way he interacted. I was impressed by that. It wasn't hollow."

As the session broke up, Winston hung back to talk to McColl. Later, when Winston got home, he found he still had more to say. He sat down and wrote a 1,200-word email, addressed it to Pugh, and asked him to forward it to McColl. In it, Winston related a personal experience to explain why people like him found themselves wary of interactions with police. Too often, the outcomes are far from what is expected.

"Black and brown people, in particular, exist in a legacy where law enforcement criminalizes people for normal human behavior," Winston wrote McColl. "The very presence of law enforcement in black and brown communities signals the state's desire to detain, strip rights, and ultimately kill a member of that society. When I say kill, though it does seem to happen far too often, I do say it with some figurative intent."

He continued, "Stories of people calling the police for help only to find themselves arrested, beaten, or killed were all too common growing up. One of the only methods that black and brown people seem to have to stop [themselves] from being criminalized by law enforcement is to not cooperate with them."

Winston got an immediate reply. "Braxton, Thanks. Let's have breakfast."

They met at Eddie's Place, a diner with a breakfast-to-lunch menu. Tucked into the corner of a suburban strip mall, the location isn't far from McColl's home, and it suited Winston, too, as his son was attending nearby Providence Day School. Winston coached lacrosse and football there and supplemented his school pay with assignments as a freelance sports videographer. He was working for the Charlotte Hornets one night and got a chance to meet Patrick Ewing, one of his all-time heroes. He says the only other person who ever made him weak in the knees was Hugh McColl. Ten years earlier, when he was a student at Davidson College, he had written a paper about McColl. He set out to profile a rapacious and heartless corporate raider. Instead, he discovered a man with a soul.

Winston was born in North Carolina and raised in New York City, where his father was a firefighter and his mother a schoolteacher. He ended up at an expensive prep school thanks to a grant from philanthropist Michael Bloomberg. Davidson met his college requirements: it was located in a warmer climate, he could continue to play football, and it was among the academically elite institutions in the country. The relationship soured after he got to North Carolina. He dropped out, then negotiated a return and picked up a degree in anthropology in 2007. "I grew as a person. I learned a lot," he would later allow. "I really do owe just about everything to my Davidson experience."

Over breakfast, Winston and McColl began a conversation that continues today. Though some of the topics they covered Winston later described as "cringe-worthy," the two men discussed tough racial issues and the mundane alike. A few weeks after their first meeting, Winston decided he was going to run for a seat on the city council. McColl was the first person he called for advice. He got encouragement and his first campaign pledge. By the time Winston reached some prospective supporters, especially those whose contributions made campaigns like his run smoothly, he discovered McColl had already spoken on his behalf. He'd make a call and be told, "Oh, yeah. I've talked to Hugh." When the votes were counted in November, Braxton Winston, the street protestor—the one with the long hair and his fist in the air—became the newest at-large member of the city council. Only one other candidate on the ballot that day received more votes.

This little city council race gained national attention. Writer Michael Graff reported on the unlikely pair, included a photo of the young Black man standing head and shoulders above a gray-headed white man in a business suit, and sent if off to *Politico*, an online news magazine with a national readership. The headline read: "Hugh McColl's Last Great Investment."

David Taylor runs the Gantt Center for African-American Arts + Culture, housed in a striking concept building at the edge of Uptown Charlotte's arts complex. Hugh and Jane McColl gave $1 million and Hugh chaired the campaign that helped open the place in 2009. It kicked off about the same time as the city was coming to grips with the Scott shooting. Taylor found McColl's interest was real, his commitment solid. At meet-and-greet events related to the fund-raising campaign, where some big names passed through the crowd quickly and then headed for the door, Taylor said he watched McColl circulate among a diverse congregation that was brought together on the center's behalf. "He was genuinely wanting to hear from people, to talk to people," Taylor said. "Hugh was learning and teaching himself and learning through others about how he could help his city be better, and in order to do that he needed to understand all of his citizens, I think in many ways—particularly the African American community, but I think other folks of color as well. I think it's about how he can impact them, and I think he knew the city needed leadership."

Chapter Eight
A Second Legacy

IT WAS just past midday, and Hugh McColl finally had a chance to gather his thoughts. His crowded morning had started with a 7:30 meeting of the Champions that went until past 9:00. Before he got away, he had a pocket full of business cards from men who wanted some of his time. Then it was on to a one-on-one with a friend who outlined his plans for rolling out Champions-like groups all across the city. Now, he was on the phone with a successful entrepreneur who was updating him on the latest prospects for opening a child development center in the decidedly poor and locally historic African American neighborhood called Paradise just across the state line in Fort Mill, South Carolina.

McColl, who turned eighty-five in the summer of 2020, says people tend to write off the elderly once they move into their ninth decade. The eighties are said to be the time when those with snow on the mountain are seen, not heard. Yet he is seldom still and manages complicated affairs, handling extended conversations with clarity and reasonable recall for a man of his years. He struggles from time to time to find the right word, or a name, but only because he values the virtue of precision. He's never been sloppy with language.

McColl had signed on to lead a campaign to raise $500 million in aid of Atrium

Health System's plans. He's available, now that he's done helping bring in $50 million to jump-start an affordable housing initiative in the city. Out of the Atrium project will come a Charlotte campus for Wake Forest University's Bowman Gray School of Medicine, the prize from a dinner he had hosted the year before welcoming people from the Winston-Salem school to town. He's also lobbying the University of North Carolina at Chapel Hill to open a campus of the Kenan-Flagler Business School in Charlotte.

There has never been what might be called slack time in McColl's life. Indeed, once he logged three-quarters of a century, he seemed to apply an even greater sense of urgency. His assistant, Paula Washam, regularly updates a daily schedule he keeps in a loose-leaf notebook that's never far from hand. He claims that he doesn't go looking for things to do. Rather, opportunities find him. As a result, he spends much of his time talking and working with people who begin as strangers but usually end up as good friends. At any given time, his disciples, who are usually half his age, may include as many as a dozen or so aspiring businessmen, nearly all of whom are African Americans. For them, it is a once-in-a-lifetime shot at being part of what one of them called McColl's "second legacy."

Everyone wants a piece of a man who once figured irrelevancy was the likely companion to retirement. He believed there would come a time when people at Bank of America would stop taking his calls. When that happened, he'd fade into the background, little more than a portrait on the wall, just another former CEO. Yet, twenty years on, he still has the ability to move people to do things, even big things. He remains one person in Charlotte whose call can convene a meeting of the city's most influential and resourceful civic and corporate leaders, says his friend Michael Marsicano at the Foundation For The Carolinas. "I think he learned that his influence was not just by the seat he held," said Marsicano. "It was by the man that he was and all that he had done for so many and in so many different subject areas. He just had all this capital with people to keep going, and he's led ever since."

Certainly, he comes to his present situation well-armed. McColl is a wealthy man, and he shares his money with the community. There is not much he and his family have not underwritten, from new costumes for the ballet to the affordable housing project undertaken by his church. His contacts within the community are unmatched, at least among those of a certain age. And they are still taking his calls at the Bank of America, where his emeritus status carries considerable weight. Hugh McColl sightings continue to be noteworthy.

His reach extends well beyond Charlotte. A few years back McColl discovered that a hacker was stealing his monthly Social Security payment. He put in a call to the regional Social Security Administration office to report the theft. After spending fifty-eight minutes on hold, he got cut off. Thoroughly disgusted, he called the White House and told his tale to Valerie Jarrett, one of President Barack Obama's senior advisers. "I said, 'Would you do me favor and get them to answer the phone?' She said, 'I'll do better than that. I'll get them to call you right away.' Sure enough, Jane and I had gotten on the airplane to fly to Florida when the phone rings. It's the head of the Social Security. It's amazing how quick you get things fixed when you start at the top."

Lots of people have money. Lots of people with money know people in high places. Not everybody can equal McColl's third chit: a spot at the top of the pecking order at Augusta National Golf Club. When Marsicano's people were trying to persuade a renowned economist and Nobel laureate from the University of Chicago to accept a speaking engagement at an event in Charlotte, McColl allowed the hosts to dangle a day at Augusta as a bribe. The professor agreed and brought a friend. That's how McColl, a C student in economics at UNC back in the 1950s, ended up dining with two internationally recognized economists, both of them receivers of Nobel honors, in the clubhouse at Augusta.

McColl's nonplussed by it all. "They use me. And I let them." As a student of leadership, he says his status can be ephemeral. "I think people impute power to you, and that helps you get a lot done if you don't use it too much. Power is a wasting asset, and you should try not to use it, if you can help it, because you are burning up something that won't come back." More likely, he says, his influence is underwritten by a lifetime of responding, often in generous fashion, to those who have asked him for favors. "Theoretically, there are a lot of tickets out there."

Academics say McColl has "social capital." It's another name for power but sounds a bit softer. Whatever it's called, a recent community-wide study says its scant use in Charlotte is one of the abiding crosscurrents—racial segregation is the other—that is inhibiting individual opportunity and economic advancement, especially for people of color. To enjoy a better life, people need mentors and role models, someone who can lend a hand. "What they call social capital," McColl says, "really is access, the ability to gain access, and sharing that access with people."

McColl is well versed in the art. He spent a career leveraging real capital to expand opportunities for his corporate customers and at the same time building a banking franchise that gobbled up competitors from coast to coast. But what he is engaged in these days is not a zero-sum game. It's designed to create win-wins. The critical ingredients are a capacity to listen, to be available as a resource, and to put faith in your fellow man. Local movers and shakers, and those who want to

> From the ballet to affordable housing, there is not much he and his family have not underwritten.

The McColl Family: Seated, L-R: Luther Lockwood, Jane McColl Lockwood, Jane McColl, Hugh McColl Jr, John McColl, Lee McColl Standing, L-R: Luke Lockwood, Jane B. Lockwood, Thomas Lockwood, Tanner McColl, Renee McColl, Hugh McColl III, Hugh McColl IV, John McColl, Duncan McColl, Virginia McColl be in that group, now lobby for his imprimatur on their pet projects.

McColl operates an equal-opportunity clearinghouse. One of his neighbors, part of the southeast Charlotte country club set, was looking for a project where she and her friends could invest their time and money and make a difference. He put her in touch with Communities in Schools, a program using some of McColl's money whose CEO had asked him for introductions to just that sort of relationship. The result was a successful fund-raiser. "I connected two women, both white, but both doing good work—one of them trying to do good work and one of them doing good work—and it's making something happen," he said one morning.

McColl is especially keen on projects that create jobs. A steady job leads to a better life. It can mean a home of one's own and the independence to use one's wealth to build a business or educate a child. That's made him a fan of Ric Elias, the Puerto Rican transplant and the founder of Red Ventures. As part of Elias's payback to a city where he has become a wealthy man, he created a unique program to pay teenagers while training them for well-paying tech jobs and opportunities for further education. His portfolio includes college scholarships for DACA kids. A fan of McColl's, Elias invited him to dinner at his mansion and then to the Red Venture campus in Rock Hill, South Carolina, to talk to his employees about the elements of leadership.

"Now we are working on things we are passionate about," Elias said. McColl helped him with plans for three training centers by interpreting the unwritten protocols of charitable financing and engaging the local bureaucracy. Charlotte's a city where reciprocity rules, McColl advised. Give here. Get there. Collaborate. Don't take all the credit for yourself. He knew which handles to pull, which buttons to push, whose number to call. "What's unique," said Elias, "is how he is able to easily connect with all parts of the community. He is a titan. There is not even a number two in Charlotte."

Building affordable housing first attracted McColl's attention forty years ago when NCNB was developing Third Ward, the southwest quadrant of Uptown. He was back at it decades later after Laura Clark and others from Renaissance West Initiative paid him a visit and asked him to help raise $15 million to build and equip RWI's child development center. RWI is Charlotte's purpose-built community, an intentional combination of public and private investment in mixed-income housing for families and the elderly, all together on a campus that includes the children's center and a K-through-8 charter school. It sits on ground once occupied by Boulevard Homes, considered Charlotte's most desperate public housing project. (Two police officers were killed there in the early 1990s. It was pulled down in 2011.)

Atlanta's East Lake Village, the nation's first such community, was developed by Tom Cousins, McColl's former board member and golfing mate from Augusta. With support from NationsBank, East Lake's first corporate sponsor, Cousins turned Atlanta's worst aggregation of public housing into a model of publicly subsidized living.

Charlotte's Renaissance West, smaller than Atlanta's East Lake, aims to do the same. In this planned neighborhood of apartments and town homes, some rent for market rate while others are subsidized. Charlotte-Mecklenburg Schools, in partnership with RWI, co-sponsors the charter school. The child development center across the way followed in 2017. All told, $100 million in public and private funds is invested in a plot of land where everyone had about given up hope of seeing anything good.

McColl had agreed to a limited role as honorary chair, but when the campaign's chair became ill it didn't take much to convince him to pick up the slack. He was a believer and familiar with both the geography and the concept. He understood that a strong, fair society requires a good job, a good education, and a good place to live. Renaissance was doing something to help some of Charlotte's neediest achieve all three.

Clark was working her way up through the ranks of Charlotte's nonprofits when she became RWI's CEO in 2013. Some of her mentors discouraged her from taking the job. "They said, 'It's never going to happen. It's a pipe dream.' And I did it anyway. So to have somebody like Hugh McColl [step in], it really meant a lot, and it turned a lot of people's opinions around." As she accompanied McColl on fund-raising calls she learned from a master. "As a young woman leader, taking on this huge project, there was so much I didn't know, but he's very clear that he wants to support women and minorities in leadership roles. Having him standing beside me as a woman in leadership is something I don't think should go unnoticed. I think there are other women leaders in the community that would say the same thing."

RWI is where McColl met Dionne Nelson. Nelson, the Black woman with the Harvard MBA, prompted McColl's public confession about his innate racial bias. RWI hired her firm to oversee the residential core of the project. "I think what resonates is his commitment to do what's right," Nelson says. "And I think that transcends a lot of different things; do what's right in changing a neighborhood to make it a better place for people to live, to make sure that young children that are in poverty can grow up and transcend that poverty. [Also] do what's right and support an African American entrepreneur who was trying to build and grow a business. If all he wanted to do was invest in housing or invest in affordable housing, he didn't have to do it with us, right? But I do believe that directly or indirectly, his support of our work is another layer of that same desire to do what's right, set a precedent, to tell a different story."

"What resonates is his commitment do to what's right."
—Dionne Nelson

Ron Leeper's construction firm built the senior living apartments at Renaissance West—the same Ron Leeper who nearly forty years earlier educated Hugh McColl on the disparities of Charlotte's west side. Leeper left the city council in the late 1980s and a few years later was drafted by McColl to create Charlotte's only minority-owned general contracting firm. In order for that to happen, McColl paid half of Leeper's salary while he apprenticed at an established outfit. McColl then helped get him started with a loan and jobs that paid enough to keep him whole. In 1994, McColl picked Leeper's firm to build Charlotte's Uptown transportation center, a project designed by Harvey Gantt.

The center opened in December 1996 at the foot of NationsBank's new tower. Passengers who used to wait curbside at Trade and Tryon for city buses, in fair weather or foul, now loaded and unloaded, safe and dry, under an open-air transit concourse with a glass ceiling four stories overhead. Restrooms were nearby, as were a police substation, a medical clinic, fast food, and an ATM. The completion of the transportation center meant that Charlotte had another award-winning building where form and function satisfied basic civic and social interests. "I am so damn proud of that transportation center," McColl said. "I've said I'm proud of my tower, but I really think that the transportation center may be the best thing I ever did for this city. It's amazing."

In 2019, when the RWI senior apartments were just another photo of company projects on Leeper's office wall, he added a coda to his McColl story. His firm had recently been awarded a major public project, and he was ensuring that every outfit involved with it included at least one pre-apprentice slot paying a minimum of $13 an hour. Employers were to select their hires from job-training nonprofits in Charlotte. "He invested in me, so I am investing in others," Leeper said. "You find somebody that just needs some guidance, some instruction, some encouragement, that's your pay it forward.

"I think Hugh really believes that for Charlotte to be what he wants it to be, and believes it has the capacity to be, that a lot of people have to be around the table contributing in a meaningful way," Leeper said. "I'm not really sure why other people don't get what Hugh obviously got.

"Even today, when I have the occasion to tell this story about Hugh paying half of my salary, I say, 'You could probably talk to a thousand people, and you probably wouldn't have ten of them to tell you that Hugh ever told about it.' It's extraordinary that somebody does something like that. That is absolutely unique and special. And then not feel the need to boast about it to everybody you come in contact with. He's a unique human being that probably you'd have to dig really deep to find more stories like this, but I'm sure there are plenty of them."

McColl's pay-it-forward admonition remains part of the deal he makes with those he draws into his circle, including James Scruggs. The two met over dinner, at the home of a mutual friend who brought six Black entrepreneurs and their wives together with the McColls, Hugh and Jane, at her home. Sonja Nichols chose the diners from a list of businessmen she knew who had established a record but who needed a boost to take the next step to move ahead and realize their potential.

After finishing at the University of Virginia, Scruggs began his career at Bank of America just as McColl was heading into retirement. Seven years later, Scruggs moved into real estate, first as a Realtor and then as a builder and a developer. Scruggs and

McColl have spent their time together discussing expansion options for one of Scruggs's companies, Opportunities Unlimited. His company builds and operates affordable assisted living residences in the Charlotte suburbs for families of moderate means whose loved ones suffer from Alzheimer's and dementia.

"The only thing Hugh is asking from us is to do the same thing, reach back and take the next person to the next level," said Scruggs. "I am part of his second legacy. There is not enough of that going on in Charlotte."

The two meet and talk periodically, usually over lunch at 300 East. Scruggs ended up tailoring his plans for an expansion of Opportunities Unlimited and using income from his home building to underwrite the project rather than chasing investors. Scruggs, like others, discovered McColl was more than just talk. One midwinter evening in 2020 he was part of a crowd celebrating the arrival of Truist, the newest big bank in town. In the room with Scruggs were city officials, civic leaders, and business executives such as Brian T. Moynihan from Bank of America; David Tepper, the owner of the Carolina Panthers; the president of Queens University; and about two hundred others from Charlotte's top echelon. McColl had seen that Scruggs and two others were on the invitation list.

"These guys are really smart," McColl said. "and these people should know them. But they don't have access. I can give a lot of them access. It didn't take a whole hell of a lot [to get this done]. One of them said, 'I'd never meet these people if it weren't for you.' And, of course, the answer is he's right."

Another in a recent "class" at McColl Business U. is Robert Mackey. They met when the former NFL linebacker settled into the seat beside McColl at one of the early meetings of the Champions. McColl liked the way Mackey chimed in during that morning's discussion over the removal of Confederate statues and remembrances. Mackey questioned just how far society should go in cleansing the South of reminders of its racial history. He said he knew his family name was there at the command of the man who enslaved his forbearers years ago. Yet Mackey men had carried that name through two world wars, the Great Depression, and Vietnam, and he wasn't about to change it. Mackey argued it was time to move on to more important topics. He and McColl later explored that idea over a meal.

Mackey and McColl—a hundred pounds lighter and nearly a foot shorter—draw curious looks from other diners when they settle into a booth together at 300 East. Mackey, who left football for business after a year, eventually landed in Morgan Stanley's sports entertainment division. Mackey was leaning on McColl for advice on how to proceed with a project of his in Paradise, South Carolina. This Black community, on the edge of Fort Mill, had been home to a cluster of families for generations. Mackey had plans for a community center where a team of social workers and teachers could use their talents to help Black students threatened with expulsion from schools. McColl has put a six-figure donation into the project and set about helping him find a match from other donors. Together they are hoping this first project might lead to something even more transformative for the neighborhood. Mackey has even investigated the prospects of a purpose-built community like Renaissance West for Paradise.

Two years after their first meeting, McColl was still advising Shaun Corbett at LuckySpot Barbershop. Corbett's expansion plans in the summer of 2020 included a second shop at a Walmart twenty-five miles west of Charlotte in Gastonia and another, planned for the summer of 2021, in a store just outside the gates of Fort Jackson in Columbia, South Carolina. Corbett and Walmart had settled on a list of about two dozen more potential locations. Corbett was preparing for a tutorial in franchising arranged by McColl with his colleagues at Falfurrias when the social and work restrictions prompted by the Covid-19 pandemic darkened offices across the city.

Businesses closed. Charlotte's office towers emptied. The region shed 70,000 jobs overnight. Workers were furloughed, while the lucky ones were consigned to working at home. That included the armies of workers at the Bank of America Corporate Center. It did not take long for the fragile place some held in the local economy to become apparent. A pop-up city of a hundred-plus tents spread out on public and private land within the shadow of the high-rise buildings on Tryon Street. This wasn't the only encampment. Two others were not that far away.

The pandemic brought McColl up short, too. The threat of a fatally infectious disease tends to focus attention when you are approaching the age of eighty-five. Hugh and Jane took precautions seriously. Even family members wore masks when they were in close proximity. Ever restless, Hugh maintained his morning walks on a multi-mile route around his neighborhood. He occupied some of his time staying in touch by telephone with those managing joint projects. In-person meetings were out of the question, so he settled for virtual sessions on Zoom or FaceTime, anathema for one who thrives on personal contact.

Nonetheless, he pushed on. "Every day I was doing something in the Black community, mainly with young, successful, or on the-way-to-success young Blacks, trying to help them with using my connections to get them capital, get them loans. [One thing] I was working on was creating an investment pool to provide capital, as opposed to loans, to existing Black businesses that are already successful but need a second wave of capital to move to the next tier.

"I've pretty much become convinced that the only way out of these problems we have is to create Black capitalism and to create jobs. If you give someone a job that he makes money in, he gets pride, he gets the ability to buy his own house, he gets the ability to educate his own children, and everybody's better off. So what I'm concentrating on now almost exclusively, I'll call it Black capitalism."

A group in Atlanta wanted his advice on forming a Black-owned bank. McColl told his six closest protégés in Charlotte to pick one thing he could do on their behalf. He found working capital for one. Another of his mentees ended up as an early client of a new company that McColl and his former partner, David Vorhoff, had begun organizing before the pandemic disrupted business. After a temporary lull the new enterprise, designed to link borrowers looking for money with lenders looking for customers, moved into the final stages of development.

As deeply unsettling as the pandemic was, nothing compared to the jolt to the nation's psyche that arrived over Memorial Day weekend when a Black man, George Floyd, died under the knee of a white police officer in Minneapolis, Minnesota. The protests against police violence that followed and the marches that spread across the nation invigorated and revived the Black Lives Matter movement like nothing had before. McColl's concerns about the seeds for revolution that he had talked about only months before now began to look very real. Yet different, too.

The 2020 response didn't just come from Blacks. Substantial numbers of whites joined them in the streets. Where in 2016, Charlotte's troubles had been concentrated mainly on the streets in the center of the city, one Sunday afternoon in 2020 hundreds of people left Uptown bearing signs and carried their protest for change right into the heart of wealthy Myers Park, where they were met with cheers from neighbors with Black Lives Matter signs in their front yards. Had McColl known visitors were on the way, he said, he would have been out there with his granddaughter, Jane, who had encouraged him to walk behind her wheelchair.

This new awakening brought calls to McColl from whites who were wise to what he had been doing for the past few years. People asked for help in connecting with Black entrepreneurs. A trustee at one school asked him to help the college find a Black money manager to handle a portion of its investment portfolio. "I said to my Black friends, we're never going to have an opportunity of where the market is more attuned to doing something. Now is the time to ask for things, for help from people who otherwise have not been interested. Now they can do that. The timing is good."

So many dials were being reset. "The challenge is that a lot of what we thought was important six months ago is not important today," McColl said. "Housing is still important, but it's not as important as health care. That's the number one. It's a fact that we're getting more people dying that are poor, who are forced into close living quarters and unable to obtain separation, and who don't get enough primary health care.

"It's a movement that has legs under it. But, of course, you have to take it to the next step. What change is it that you want? We want the justice system to change and quit sentencing everybody to jail for minor crimes. We want illegal search and seizure—that is, stopping people for no reason other than being Black, [which is] a violation of the Fourth Amendment—to cease. Those things can be dealt with. But the underlying principle is one of people's individual hearts and minds, and that's much more difficult. We don't really need new laws so much. We just need to treat Black people in the way that they're entitled to as American citizens."

At the same time, an incident occurred to serve as a vivid reminder that the very issue that engaged McColl with the Champions, which had connected him to a young politician named Braxton Winston and had led to so much more—the question of trust between Black citizens and police—remained stuck at an impasse.

A midnight shooting spree in mid-June, 2020, on Beatties Ford Road in West Charlotte took place not far from where volunteers had gathered twenty years earlier to build some of the McColl Habitat houses. The large gathering was part of a weekend-long Juneteenth celebration and included many witnesses who saw multiple shooters fire on a crowd, killing four people. Ten others were hit by gunfire or by cars racing from the scene. Six weeks after the incident no one had come forward to tell police what they had seen or heard. Even pleas from family members of one of the victims went unanswered.

Which comes back to the question, why does Hugh McColl keep answering phone calls and rising early every fourth Wednesday to drink lukewarm coffee and share himself at the Champions sessions? Why does he bother? Why not do something else? The ranch is always there.

"I'm doing it like I always do things," McColl says, "because I can. I guess I should examine my own motivation and whether I am doing this because I feel guilty of being privileged and white. I think not. It's just late in life, and I've gotten interested in trying to help people level the playing field."

> I'm going to fix things that I can fix. I'm going to work on what I can work on."
>
> —Hugh McColl

"In the last part of my life, I'm going to fix things that I can fix," he said. "I realize I'm not going to change the world, but I can change the part of it I'm rubbing up against. That's what I'm trying to do. I'm going to work on what I can work on."

His friend and pastor Bob Henderson put it differently. "This is noblesse oblige. He has social capital, he has money, he has influence, and he wants to impact the world for good. I think it's fascinating. I think it's beautiful. He could be someplace on the Riviera and not worry about a barbershop in Charlotte. In the last eight to ten years, he has found a new horizon to live with purpose and energy, and he's embracing it. He's bringing his incredible intellect, his keen observation, his social consciousness, and everything he has to bear to try to make the world a better place. It's exciting to see."

A good example of what Henderson saw in McColl is embodied in a project bearing McColl's imprint. His plans for a Black enterprise private equity fund were finally complete. As the new year arrived Charlotte was learning about Bright Hope Capital LLC, whose principals were McColl and two of Charlotte's Black millionaires, Malcomb Coley and Lloyd Yates. Coley was managing partner at EY Charlotte; Yates was a former executive vice president of Duke Energy who was president of the Carolinas region before his retirement in 2019. The three had taken more than a year to arrange the particulars of their plans that also included participation from Bank of America as part of its $1 billion commitment to economic and racial equality.

In the years ahead the three have plans to bring Bright Hope's resources to bear on proven minority-owned businesses stymied in place due to a shortage of money to expand and grow. "We're trying to make a difference," McColl explained. "We are trying to provide equity. We are not trying to take over their business. We are not going to do that. What we are trying to do is make them successful and help them get to where they can secure better financing. It is doing what we have been doing for white businesses for many years. [This time], it is working to build Black capital."

A flurry of news accounts took notice of the racial composition of Bright Hope's principals, majority Black, as well as its declared mission to help Black- and brown-owned companies build diverse workspaces and offer secure jobs with ample benefits and living wages. Nothing like it existed in the Carolinas. Equally as exciting for McColl, and largely overlooked in this coverage, was a declaration by the firm's creators, all of whom had ponied up a million dollars or more, to forsake any claim to the profits. Revenue from Bright Hope's deals would be used to increase the resources of Bright Hope not the investors.

"This is not charitable," McColl insisted. "This is business. We are not trying to give away money. We are trying to make money and help people make money. It makes money and we reinvest it and make things happen."

Coley told Tony Mecia at *Charlotte Ledger*, an online business publication, that Bright Hope was "transformative. You have these minority businesses that tend to be underserved and marginally capitalized. Our focus was how do we take our financial capital and social capital and prop these companies up to scale. If we do that, everybody benefits. And hopefully it inspires some young kid to say, 'You know what? I can grow a business.'"

Bright Hope's inaugural deal, closed on December 30, 2020, had a special meaning for McColl. He and his partners purchased 75 percent ownership of Ron Leeper's construction company, the same outfit that he had helped Leeper organize a quarter century earlier. The new president and owner of the balance of RJ Leeper Construction Company was James Mitchell, a Black man and at-large member of the Charlotte City Council. The deal insured that Leeper's firm would remain one of the leading minority-owned businesses in the city, an outcome that McColl had been helping his old friend try to arrange for more than a year.

"Ron is going to have a great life," McColl said. "He gets to retire. When he came back from Vietnam, he was just a broke Black Panther. By enabling a Black man to buy his business, we are saving a black-owned business and we also enable the man who ran it his day to sit on the beach in the sunset with a handsome net worth. If he had had to sell it to a white owner, all of that Black enterprise would have been for naught."

Within Bright Hope's portfolio was a range of choices for what the principals hoped would include at least in a dozen projects in its first year. Immediately waiting in the wings, was a merger bringing together the talents of McColl's barber friends, Shaun Corbett and the Johnson brothers, Damian and Jermaine. The day after the Leeper purchase was announced, McColl was at the barber college the Johnsons run from a building on Charlotte's west side. With him for the day was David Sheffer, a protégé from the McColl Partners days. Sheffer was there to talk about franchising. They started out at the school where McColl circulated among the students standing by their chairs, chatting with each about their ambitions. Outfitted in his trademark dark jeans and wearing a Marine Corps ballcap, McColl spent a little extra time beside the chair of a barber-to-be who was a more recent member of the Corps. McColl's casual appearance belied the difference he was going to be making in their lives. It wasn't until sometime later, when Damian Johnson returned without McColl that the students learned the consequence of their morning guest.

Damian Johnson said Sheffer's introduction to franchising was eye-opening as he explained that the barbers' proposed business model wasn't all that different from MyEyeDr.com, an online creation of Sheffer's that was a multi-billion-dollar deal providing eye care. The plans afoot call for Corbett and the Johnsons to combine resources and place graduates of the Johnson's barber school in the shops Corbett will be opening in Walmart as well as future NoGrease! locations in strip centers and shopping malls where the Johnsons' connections are equally strong.

Big deals, small deals would all have the same theme, building Black capital. What Bright Hope was doing was nothing more than what bankers like McColl had done for years. "If these were white guys somebody would have put them together a long time ago. Somebody would have. But nobody thinks of putting Black people together and doing a deal.

"People say where are you going to find opportunity," he continued. "Hell, I am covered up with opportunity. If putting out all the money represents success, we will have success. And we will get it back with a reasonable return, and we will reinvest it."

In the spring of 2019, the director of the Echo Foundation in Charlotte, the one that had presented its Award Against Indifference to McColl some years back, asked him to speak at the foundation's annual meeting. It had recently completed a project titled "Charlotte: A Tale of Two Cities" and released an anthology of essays, news accounts, and academic studies in response to the Harvard/UC Berkeley study that ranked Charlotte at the bottom for upward mobility among the nation's cities.

McColl found himself before an appreciative audience. Those on hand included old allies and partners on projects all around the city. Present were contemporaries like Harvey Gantt and Rolfe Neill, the former newspaper publisher, who used to walk around Uptown Charlotte with McColl and imagine what could be. Charlotte's elite was seating two generations deep. Even better, those being honored that evening were friends receiving the same award presented him years earlier. One was a former colleague from Bank of America.

McColl had been asked to tailor his remarks to the "two cities" theme. Finding something to say wasn't hard to do; the topic had been part of his repertoire for three decades or more. As much as he and the others had done to make the city more fair, more equitable, more livable, and more welcoming, the gaps in access to education, health care, housing, and more remained broad. McColl said he'd read a recent newspaper article declaring that such a state of affairs was discouraging to lifelong Charlotte residents. It was discouraging to him, too. "I've always thought that if we all tried to live personal lives as free from prejudice as possible that social progress would naturally follow," he allowed.

McColl is comfortable behind a microphone. It was his night, and looking back on the occasion a few weeks later, he mused that it may have been the best speech he had delivered. He continued with his theme.

"When we fail to bring opportunity to all our citizens, our entire city suffers. When we fail to develop the talents and leadership potential of all our citizens, we neglect our most vital resource as a community. Our people.

"To put it in terms appropriate to our city's past, it's like we're sitting on a gold mine, and no one remembered to bring a shovel."

(McColl's collaborator on the speech, Todd Rubenson, says he might have borrowed that last line from Gantt. But it suited McColl fine.)

"I believe we need a new governance model that forces every decision about our future as a city—public decisions and private decisions—to run through the filter of this question: How will this decision help spread opportunity to the areas and the people of our city who need it more?"

He was preaching to the choir, but without any in the audience aware he was laying the foundation for what James Scruggs called his second legacy that would eventually help Ron Leeper see his business continue as a leading minority-owned enterprise or secure a berth for man learning a trade be able to buy a home, raise a family, or even start a business of his own. On that night, he was presenting the essence of the two decades that had passed since his retirement.

"When we can truly look one another in the eye and believe and trust that we are doing this, bringing all our neighbors into our story of growth and prosperity, only then will we know that our 'Tale of Two Cities' is becoming a tale of one city, one community united in purpose and spirit."

ACKNOWLEDGMENTS

HUGH McCOLL made this book possible, allowing me to enter his personal space at a point in his life when his time is entirely his own. It helped, I think, that we weren't strangers because of our earlier work together. Nonetheless, it took some getting used to one another. Thankfully, my reward was candor and honesty. I am deeply grateful and honored by the opportunity to tell this story.

McColl's hospitality was the founder of this feast, so to speak, he also made possible introductions to others who were equally as generous with their time. For example, Brenda Suits, a former co-worker and his "Habitat wife," tutored me on the inside story of the two hundred plus houses built in McColl's name across the country. She coordinated the travel and then worked side-by-side on those building sites as a regular member of a Bank of America team from Charlotte that included Juan Lozano, the man who provided a cache of photographs from those days.

Sy Pugh invited me to some Champions meetings, the monthly gathering of men that includes McColl. This is a group of Black and white men who talk openly and honestly about race and culture as they examine ways to learn about themselves and each other. McColl has been a faithful participant since its founding more than six years ago.

I am indebted to Michael Graff, a keen observer and talented writer at *Charlotte Agenda*, for photos of Shaun Corbett, the subject of Graff's articles. Likewise, Matthew Tyndall at Braxton Winston's campaign office shared some of his work.

During this journey of discovery, more than fifty people favored me with their stories and experiences. Some have known McColl for half a century while others only met him long after he had moved into retirement. The comparison of their insights over the decades was testimony to McColl's trust in the capacity and resilience of his fellow man. Fortunately, these interviews were completed before a national health emergency sent us all into sequestration.

Paula Washam and Carolyn Hubbard, her predecessor at Falfurrias Capital, kept my work on track and were ready with phone numbers and contact information. Paula maintains McColl's schedule and I learned early on from Carolyn that if my sessions weren't on the boss's calendar that is updated almost daily then our meetings wouldn't take place, no matter what McColl and I might have arranged on the side.

I also am grateful to Jo Ann Young, the widow of Ross Yockey, and her daughter, Beth Yockey Jones, who retrieved the transcripts of Yockey's conversations with McColl for his 1999 biography McColl, *The Man with America's Money*. These sessions proved helpful in creating the backdrop for this account of McColl's life.

John Pietsch and Bill Dantos made it possible to shoot Chas Fagan's portrait of McColl that graces the cover of this book. Pulling everything together was Leslie Rindoks at Lorimer Press.

My thanks and appreciation to all who made this book possible.

About the Author

Howard E. Covington Jr. is a native of North Carolina and has been writing history and biography, primarily about North Carolina people and topics, for more than thirty-five years. His work as an independent historian followed a newspaper career that included assignments as a reporter and an editor in Jacksonville, Florida, and Charlotte and Greensboro, North Carolina, where he now makes his home. In 1981 an investigative series he created and co-wrote for the *Charlotte Observer* on health hazards in the textile industry received the Pulitzer Prize for Public Service. Two of his books have won awards from the North Caroliniana Society and North Carolina Literary and Historical Association.

INDEX

300 East 57, 133, 134

A
Adopt a Home (Habitat program) 23
Alexander, W. S. 15–16
Alinsky, Saul 19, 49
Alpha Mill 23
American Trust Company 33
Andreozzi, Eric 34, 37
Armando's Boot Company 92–93 (*see also*: Rios, Armando Duarte)
Arthur Anderson 49
art (personal interest) 6, 48, 51, 86, 91, 95
Arts and Sciences Council (ASC) 71, 73, 74, 75
Atrium Health System 76, 125–126
Augusta National Golf Club 6, 41, 42–45, 53, 85, 127, 130
Award Against Indifference 49–50, 140

B
Ballantyne Resort 48–49
Baltimore Afro-American 109
Banc of America Securities 34
Bank of America v, ix, 3–5, 8–9, 11–12, 17, 19–22, 26, 28, 30–31, 33–37, 42, 52–55, 57, 60–66, 68–71, 73, 78–79, 82, 99, 105, 126–127, 132–134, 138, 140
Bank of America Corporate Center v, 9, 19, 34, 35, 57, 134
Bank of America Foundation 22, 26
Bank of American Stadium 54, 114
Bank of Marlboro 107
BankAmerica 4, 19, 58
Barnett Banks 62
BB&T 37–38
Beatties Ford Road 15, 16, 17, 137
Bechtol, Ken 26
Belk (store) 109
Belk, John R. 61, 80
Belk Theater 75, 103
Bessant, Catherine 19, 20
Bethune, Mary McLeod 109
Biddle Heights (Charlotte neighborhood) 17
Black capital 138, 140
Black Lives Matter 7, 135, 136
Black Panther 111, 139
Blumenthal Center for the Performing Arts 75, 80, 82
Boatman's Bancshares 115
Bojangles' 9, 55, 57, 61, 70
Bonnefoux, Jean-Pierre 83
Booker Street 15
Boren, Nelson 90–91
Bowles, Camilla Parker 84
Bowles, Erskine 37
Bowles Hollowell Conner 37
Bowman Gray School of Medicine 126
Braswell, Kim 26
Bright Hope Capital 138–140
Brooklyn (Charlotte neighborhood) 16, 17, 23
Brown, Ed 55
Business Roundtable 5
Byrnes, James F. 109

C
C&S/Sovran 18
Caldwell Presbyterian 67
Cameron M. Harris & Co. 37
Carolina Business Review 49
Carolina Cattle Company (CCC) 99
Carolina Inn 39
Carolina Panthers 55, 81, 133
Catholic Diocese of Corpus Christi 93
Central High School 72
Central Piedmont Community College 12
Champions, the 116, 119, 120, 125, 133, 136, 137
Charlotte (magazine) 84
Charlotte Ballet 74, 81, 83, 84, 126, 128
Charlotte Business Journal 51
Charlotte City Council 7, 110, 111, 122, 131, 139
Charlotte Daily Observer 15
Charlotte Ledger 138
Charlotte-Mecklenburg Schools 130
Charlotte Observer v, 48, 54, 60, 66, 75, 79, 81, 143
Charlotte Symphony Orchestra (CSO) 48, 71, 72–75, 79–83, 87, 103
Chetty, Raj 8
childcare (NCNB) 47
Children's Defense Fund (CDF) 108, 110
Children's Theater of Charlotte 81
Christus Spohn Hospital-Kleberg 98
Cielo de Cazadores de Codorniz (see also: Quail Hunters Heaven) 88, 89, 90–91, 93
Cinergy Corporation 79
Citigroup 20, 51
Clark, Laura 129, 130
Cleghorn, John (Rev.) 67, 105, 115
Clinton, Bill (President) 18, 118
Clinton, Hillary Rodham 110
Clinton Park (Charlotte neighborhood) 16
Colaco, Philip 37
Coley, Malcomb 138
Communities in Schools 129
Community Reinvestment Act 69
Consumer Finance Protection Bureau 68
Cops & Barbers 8–9
Corbett, Shaun 1–3, 8–10, 13, 134, 139, 140
Cortes, Ernesto 49
Coulter, David 58
Countrywide Financial 61–64
Cousins, Tom 43, 130
Covenant Presbyterian Church 21, 31, 120

INDEX

Covid-19 (coronavirus) 8, 87, 134
Crutchfield, Ed 79
CSX 57
Curl, Greg 62

D

Deloitte Corporate Finance 36, 70
DeMordant, Lorin 37
de Roxlo, Guillermo S. 72
Desert of the Dead 89
Dickson, Alan 78
Dilworth (Charlotte neighborhood) 51, 57, 117
Doctors Without Borders 50
Dodd-Frank Wall Street Reform and Consumer Protection Act 68, 69
Dolby, Ed 115
Douglas International (Airport) 35, 55
Dowd, Frank, IV 61
Drakensburg Range 33
Druid Hills 30
Drury, Lynn 17, 18, 20, 21
Duffey, Patrick 97
Duke Energy 64, 79, 80, 138

E

Easley, Lynn 95
Eastover (Charlotte neighborhood) 51
Echo Foundation 49, 50, 140
Eddie's Place 121
Edelman, Marian Wright 180-109, 120
Eisenhower, Dwight (President) 43
Eisenhower Tree 43
Elias, Ric 13, 129
Elizabeth (Charlotte neighborhood) 16
Enoru, Debra Orock 77-78
EquiCredit 62-63
Excelsior Club 17
EY Charlotte 138

F

Falfurrias Capital Partners 5, 52-56, 61, 65, 70, 89, 92-93, 124
First Republic Bank 34, 69, 96
First Union National Bank 19, 37, 79
First Union Securities 34
Flagstar 55
Fleet Boston Financial Corporation 60, 61
Floyd, George 135
Forbes, Malcolm 62
Fortune 500 8
Foundation For The Carolinas 75, 81, 125, 126
Founders Hall v
Fourth Ward (Charlotte) 111, 113, 114
Fuller, Millard 41
Furniss, Rosemary 82

G

Gantt, Harvey 104, 113, 114, 131, 140, 141
[Harvey B.] Gantt Center for African American Arts + Culture 9, 123
Garella, Julie 46, 51
Gates, Bill 12, 43
Gates, Henry Louis, Jr. 49-50
Geiger, Karen 47, 48
Ghost Camp 93
Goldman Sachs 46
Grace, Charles Manuel ("Sweet Daddy," Bishop) 16
Graff, Michael 2, 84, 122
Great Recession 5, 56, 64, 65, 66, 93
Green Gate Garden 107
Grier, Jannie 30

H

Habitat for Humanity 18, 20-28, 30-33, 41, 64, 82, 137
Hagman, Larry 97
Halo Flight 98
Harris, Cameron M. (Cammie) 37

health care 34, 101, 136, 141
Henderson, Bob (Rev.) 13, 31-32, 96-97, 101, 120, 137, 138
Hinson, Pat 22, 33, 38, 77
Horlock, Frank 94
House of Prayer and Church of the Rock 16
House of Prayer for All People 17
Hubert, Bo 100-101
hunting ix, 6, 52, 92-98, 101, 101, 115, 116
Hurricane Hugo 47
Hyde Park (Charlotte neighborhood) 17

I

Immelt, Jeff 45
Independence Park 72
Industrial Areas Foundation 49

J

JP Morgan Chase and Company 40
Jarrett, Valerie 127
Jennings Street 108
Johnson, Damian 9-11, 139
Johnson, George Dean, Jr. 97
Johnson, Hootie 41, 42, 44
Johnson, Jermaine 9-11, 139
Johnson C. Smith University (formerly Biddle Institute) 15, 24

K

Kenan-Flagler Business School 126
Kenedy ranch 93, 94, 100
Kennedy, John F. (President) 67
Kochner, Bernard 50

L

LaSalle Bank 61
Laurel Street (company) 117
Lee, Bill 79-80
Leeper, Ron 110-112, 113, 131, 132
Levine, Leon 79
Lewin, Jamie 37
Lewis, Kenneth D. 57, 60, 61, 63, 64, 65, 68

INDEX

Limestone College   115
Lockwood, Jane B.   26, 128
Lockwood, Jane M.   76, 77, 128
Long, Ben   86
Lozano, Jenelle   25
Lozano, Juan   25, 26, 28, 29, 30
LuckySpot Barbershop   1–3, 12, 89, 134

M

M&A   40
Mackey, Patricia   25
Mackey, Robert   133-134
Marks, Bruce   19
Marlboro Country Club   44
Marlboro County Courthouse   109
Marlboro Training High School   108
Marsicano, Michael   75, 80, 81, 84, 126, 127
Martin, Jim   80
Martin, Joe   80
Martin, Jonathan   81
Maschal, Richard   75
Masters Tournament   42, 43
MBNA   61
McBride, Patricia   83
McColl, Duncan   128
McColl, Duncan D.   106
McColl, Frances   106–107
McColl, Gabrielle Drake   107
McColl, Hugh III   35, 77, 128
McColl, Jane   24, 25, 33, 34, 48, 50, 51, 58, 63, 67, 71, 73, 84, 75, 77, 82, 83, 84, 85, 87, 95, 96, 98, 123, 127, 128, 132, 134, 136
McColl, John   128
McColl Business U.   133
McColl Camp   92, 98
McColl Center for Art + Innovation   78, 83
McColl Fine Art   51
McColl Garella   46, 48, 51
McColl Group   35
McColl Habitat Building Project (McColl build)   20, 24, 30, 59, 137

McColl Partners   35–41, 44–46, 50–52, 57, 70, 77, 99, 139
McCrorey Heights (Charlotte neighborhood)   17
McMahan, Ed   53
Medici, Lorenzo de   48
Merrill Lynch   35, 36, 64
Mieduch, Dan   34
Mitchell, James   139
Morehead-Cain Scholar   39
Morrison, Mrs. Cameron (Sarah)   72
Moynihan, Brian T.   19, 65, 68, 79, 80, 133
Mozilo, Angelo   62, 64, 68
Myers Park (Charlotte neighborhood)   15, 136
MyEyeDr.com   39, 40, 140

N

NationsBank   4, 18–20, 22, 36–38, 42, 55, 75, 92, 94, 114, 130, 131
Neighborhood Assistance Corporation of America   19
Neill, Rolfe   79, 140
Nelson, Dionne   117–118, 131
NetJets   93
Newsome, Mary   66
Nichol, Gene   104
Nichols, Sonja   132
NoGrease!   10, 12, 140
North Carolina Children's Hospital   39
North Carolina National Bank (NCNB)   3–4, 18, 23, 34, 37, 41, 47–48, 51–52, 55, 57, 59, 61, 69, 75, 105, 110–114, 129
North Carolina Symphony Orchestra   48, 71–75, 80–82, 83, 84, 87, 103

O

Oakview Terrace   30
Obama, Barack (President)   9, 12, 64, 67, 68, 127
Odell, A. G.   114
Oken, Marc A.   52–55, 93

Opera Carolina   74, 81
Opportunities Unlimited   133
Optimist Park   23, 25
Oratorio Singers of Charlotte   82
Orr, Glenn   38
Ovens Auditorium   73–75

P

Pawleys Island   95
Payne, Billy   42
Pegram Street   25
Pilbrow, Richard   75
Pittsburgh Courier   109
Porter-Leath   28
Price Waterhouse   51, 52
Providence Day School   121
Puerto Escondido   30
Pugh, Sy   *115*, 116, 119
Putney, Kerr   9, 120, 121

Q

Quail Hunters Heaven (see also: *Cielo de Cazadores de Codorniz*)   88, 89, *90–91*, 93
Quantico   4
Queens University   21, 51, 77, 133
Quincy's Family Steakhouse   55

R

ram's head (buckle)   6, 92
Rash, Dennis   113
Red Beach   45
Red Ventures   13, 129
Redbud Street   24, 25
Reese, Addison H.   4, 36
Renaissance West Initiative (RWI)   129–132, 134
Republic Bank   34
Richardson, Jerry   54, 55, 81
Ridley, Fred S.   42
Rifkin, Jeremy   49
Rio Grande Valley   4, 92
Rio Paisano   94
Rios, Armando Duarte   92–93 (see also: Armando's Boot Company)

Rita Division 94
RJ Leeper Construction Company 139
Road2Hire 13
Roberts, Clifford 42, 43
Robicsek, Francis (Dr.) 86
Rogers, Jim 79, 80
Royal Dutch/Shell 49
Rubenson, Todd 141
Ruddick Corporation 78

S
San Juan Day 45
Sanders, D. J. 15
Scott, Keith Lamont 103, 104, 116, 123
Scruggs, James 131–133, 141
Second Ward (Charlotte neighborhood) 16, 17
segregation 107, 109, 128
Sheffer, David 39, 40–41, 42, 45, 77, 139, 140
Shiloh Baptist Church 108
six-gun 92
sixties (decade) 7, 17, 67, 69
Sloan, Temple 100
snake-guard boots 92
Sonoco Corporation 57
Sorbonne 118
South Texan of the Year 97
South Texas 6, 92, 97
South Texas Charity Weekend 97
Spangler, C. D., Jr. (Dick) 45–46, 73, 75, 78, 84
Spellman College 118
Stephens, Jack 42
Stewart Creek 16
Stickler, Bob 81–82
Storrs, Thomas I. 4, 57, 59
Stringfield, Lamar 73
Stumpf, John 68
Suits, Brenda L. 21–25, 26, 27, 31, 82–83

T
Tabernacle Baptist Church 24, 25
Taylor, David 123
Tepper, David 133
Third Ward (Charlotte neighborhood) 113, 129
Thompson, Ken 37
Thrive Campaign 84, 87
Tribble, Mary 49
Truist 133

U
United Way 81
University of North Carolina at Chapel Hill 109, 126
University of North Carolina at Greensboro 22
University of Virginia 132
University Park (Charlotte neighborhood) 17
Urban Ministry 66

V
Vandiver, Bill 112, 113
Veterans International Bridge 89
Vickers-Koch, David 26
Vorhoff, David 34, 35, 37, 38, 44, 45, 67, 135
Vorhoff, Erin 48, 99

W
Wachovia Bank and Trust Company 37, 53, 59, 63, 64, 66, 71
Wachovia Corporation 3
Walker, David 23, 26, 2
Wall, E. Craig, Jr. 97
Wall Street Journal 40, 62
Walmart 1, 2, 3, 134, 140
Walton, Curt 66
Warren, Earl 109–110
Warren-Green, Christopher 72, 82, 84, 103
Warren-Green, Jamie 82
Washam, Paula 126
Washington Heights (Charlotte neighborhood) 16, 17–18, 21, 24, 25, 26, 30
Watson, C. H. 16
Watt, Mel 124
Watts, George W. 72
Way, Charles S., Jr. 53
Wells Fargo 64, 67, 68, 71
Werry, Scott 39, 40, 50, 99
West Charlotte High School 17
Western Heights 16
Wiesel, Elie 49
Wild Horse Desert 89
William, Chris 49
Winer, Bradley 37
Winston, Braxton 7, 120–122
Wolfe, Tom 49
WorldCom 49
Wright, Arthur Jerome (Rev.) 108, 109

Y
Yale 118
Yates, Lloyd 138

Z
Zell, Sam 62

Also by Howard E. Covington Jr.

Fire & Stone: The Making of the University of North Carolina under Presidents Edward Kidder Graham and Harry Woodburn

Lending Power: How Self-Help Credit Union Turned Small-Time Loans into Big-Time Change

Henry Frye: North Carolina's First African American Chief Justice

An Independent Profession: A Centennial History of the Mecklenburg County Bar (with Marion A. Ellis)

Once Upon A City: Greensboro, North Carolina's Second Century

Lady on the Hill: How Biltmore Estate Became An American Icon

Favored By Fortune: George W. Watts and the Hills of Durham

Terry Sanford: Politics, Progress, and Outrageous Ambition (with Marion A. Ellis)

The Story of NationsBank: Changing the Face of American Banking (with Marion A. Ellis)